USBORNE TRUE STORIES

GANGSTERS

This edition published in 2007 by Usborne Publishing Ltd,
Usborne House, 83-85 Saffron Hill, London
EC1N 8RT, England.
www.usborne.com

A catalogue record for this title is available
from the British Library

Printed in Chippenham, Eastbourne, UK.

Series editors: Jane Chisholm and Rosie Dickens
Designed by Sarah Cronin
Series designer: Mary Cartwright
Illustrated by Ian McNee
Cover design by Michael Hill

JFMAMJJA OND/13 01878/03

ISBN 9780746089736

USBORNE TRUE STORIES

GANGSTERS

HENRY BROOK

CONTENTS

The ice-cold killers

The two policemen climbed out of their patrol car and checked their machine guns. It was a bitterly cold morning in Chicago, well below freezing, with a biting wind whistling off Lake Michigan. They blew on their fingers, trying to warm them, then walked over to the garage door. Once inside, they tiptoed along a narrow corridor, moving silently in the direction of the voices coming from the back.

A few hundred yards away on North Clark Street, a black sedan purred to a halt. Sitting up from his snug leather seat, the gang leader George "Bugs" Moran peered over his bodyguard's shoulder at the police car waiting outside his garage.

"Cops," he hissed. "Must be a raid. Let's get some breakfast. We'll come back in an hour and see if everything's OK."

The sedan turned noiselessly and vanished around the corner of a building. As it slid from view, three more men stepped out from the back seat of the police car. They hadn't seen Moran come and go. One of them cradled a shotgun in his arms, the other two carried machine guns. All three wore expensive suits, hand-crafted Italian leather shoes and stylish hats. Their faces were broken and scarred. They were not policemen.

In the back room of the garage, the cream of Moran's gang were playing cards and chatting, sipping coffee to ward off the cold. Frank and Peter Gusenberg were experienced gunmen, famous around the city for having tried to assassinate a rival gang-boss, Al Capone, a few months earlier. John May was a mechanic who helped with the gang's less honest business when he needed extra money: he had seven children to support. Albert Weinshank ran a "speakeasy" (an illegal bar/nightclub). James Clark was Moran's brother-in-law, and Adam Heyer handled the gang's accounts.

There was a seventh man in the room who had nothing to do with the gangster war that was raging in Chicago that year. He was Dr. Rheinhardt Schwimmer, a 29-year-old eye surgeon who liked to boast about his criminal friends. Their company made Schwimmer feel superior to his law-abiding peers. He knew that Capone had promised to destroy Moran and his gang, but he didn't consider himself to be in any danger. After all, he wasn't a gangster. He'd only stopped by at the garage to play a few hands of poker before returning to his practice.

The two policemen stepped into the room. Frank Gusenberg snaked a hand to the gun holster under his jacket, but when he noticed the uniforms he relaxed. "Don't worry boys, it's just the cops."

The policemen trained their guns on the

gangsters. "Line up against that wall," came the order. "Face first."

"Yeah, yeah, we know the drill," Frank answered in a mocking tone. "We'd better do as they say," he barked at the others.

For a second, Schwimmer wondered if he should try explaining that he was a doctor and really had to be going. But when he saw the muzzles of the guns motioning him to turn around, he decided to say nothing. The seven men lined up, hands in the air, their noses almost touching the icy bricks of the garage wall.

For a few seconds there was silence, then Frank heard the click of a leather heel on the cobbles outside. "Who's that?" he demanded. "Is there another cop out there?"

The sound of running feet echoed along the corridor from the street.

Frank was getting annoyed. He wasn't used to being pushed around by the police. There was an important shipment of Canadian whiskey arriving this morning. The boss himself would be here any minute, and he'd be furious if a few cops had interrupted the delivery.

"Officers, please," he started, slowly turning his head, "can't we come to an arrangement? If it's a question of money..."

Frank stared. The two cops had been joined by three men in expensive suits. One of the policemen dropped his cap to the ground. His knuckles were white where they gripped the trigger handle of his gun. In a flash, Frank realized these weren't real cops, but executioners. "Don't do it," he pleaded too late, as their guns began to blaze.

The assassins had been well organized and patient. They had rented an apartment opposite the garage and watched the comings and goings through its doors for weeks. They had even arranged the ruse of the whiskey shipment, posing as a Canadian gang who wanted to sell alcohol to Moran. The truck was due to arrive at 11:00am on February 14, 1929. At 10:30am, a lookout thought he saw Moran and six of his gang enter the building. He was mistaken. Weinshank, who had a similar build and height to Moran, was wrongly identified as the gang leader. The lookout rushed to the phone on the landing and made a call.

"They're here," he whispered into the receiver.

Minutes later, the stolen police car arrived with its deadly cargo of killers.

Somehow, Frank Gusenberg survived the storm of machine-gun bullets. When the real police arrived, they sped the dying gangster to the hospital and questioned him about his attackers. Gusenberg must have recognized some of the men who shot him, but he refused to talk. He died of his wounds three hours after the massacre. The only other survivor of the shooting was John May's German Shepherd dog, "Highball." When a press photographer found the animal hiding in the garage, it was shaking uncontrollably. It had listened to the roar of over 100 gunshots.

This was the worst gangland killing in criminal history. It wasn't just that seven men had been shot dead – a record number for any gang murder. But the victims were cut down in a neat, orderly line, mimicking an official execution, and the killers had shown open contempt for the authorities by daring to impersonate policemen. Newspapers around the world reported the chilling facts of the shooting, quickly dubbing it "The St. Valentine's Day Massacre." Editorials announced the reign of the violent, criminal gang, the new plague of the nation. Who were these killers who stood in defiance of the law, who took what they wanted by force and corrupted society and its values wherever they went? The violent shadow-world of the gangsters had been suddenly exposed.

Bugs Moran went into hiding. He'd had a lucky escape, but his gang was shattered. It never recovered its former strength, and the boss who once ruled north Chicago was finally reduced to robbing grocery stores in order to feed himself. He died in prison, in 1957.

No one was prosecuted for the massacre. Gangsters whispered that Capone had ordered it, but Moran had plenty of other enemies. To this day, the murders remain unsolved.

How they cracked Capone

Al Capone was working as a waiter and bouncer at the Harvard Inn when he first met Frank Galluccio. Barely out of his teens, Capone was an apprentice gangster at the time, pushy and self-confident. He also thought of himself as a lady-killer, and made the mistake of whispering a crude remark to Galluccio's sister. It almost got him killed. Galluccio's knife flashed three times and Capone's left cheek was cut to the bone, from the tip of his eyebrow to the curve of his chin. But that wasn't enough to satisfy Galluccio. He went to see New York's "boss of bosses," Lucky Luciano, and demanded that the young thug be punished. Luciano took charge of the situation, ordered Capone to apologize and the matter was forgotten. Years later, when Capone was a boss himself, he gave Galluccio a job in his gang. He respected the man who had stood up to him, even if the knife wounds had earned him a nickname he always loathed: "Scarface." But few men were ever brave enough to call him that to his face.

Capone tried to disguise his scars: he covered them in flesh-toned talcum powder and, when posing for a photograph, he always turned his right cheek to the camera lens. Late in his career he tried to present himself as a respectable Chicago businessman, but the scars were a permanent symbol of the violent truth. He was a brutal gangster, probably the world's richest at his peak. During the late 1920s, he was earning an estimated $2,000,000 a year from his empire of gambling dens and speakeasies – almost $30,000,000 in today's money. Seventy percent of the local police force took bribes from him. Judges and politicians flocked to his lavish parties. Other gangsters might have had larger gangs and criminal networks, but Capone was different: he enjoyed his fame. Even today, he is probably the person most people think of when they hear the term "gangster." Capone was a celebrity, a man about town who loved to attend opera concerts and baseball games, surrounded by his entourage of newspaper photographers and bodyguards. He was a stylish dresser. His suits were made of the finest silk and, on his little finger, he wore a diamond ring worth $50,000. His car was a giant limousine, a bulletproof Cadillac that cost $30,000 to build. Al Capone was the "King of Chicago," and he flaunted it. But he had started with nothing.

He was born Alphonse Caponi in Brooklyn, New York, on January 17, 1899. His parents were immigrants from Naples, in southern Italy, who had crossed the Atlantic after hearing stories of a paradise to be found in America. Instead of the hardships of their peasant life, the new country promised them well-paid jobs, clean houses, and good schools and hospitals for their children. They soon learned the truth: the slums of New York were filthy and dangerous, and the only work available was back-breaking and badly paid. This wasn't the kind of life Alphonse wanted. At 14, he changed his name to Al Capone, quit school and joined a notorious gang, known as "The Five Points."

Capone soon got a reputation for being a vicious street fighter who showed no mercy. It was then that he started work at the Harvard Inn, where his fighting skills came in handy when dealing with awkward customers. But a year later the police were looking for him in connection with an unsolved murder. Capone needed to get out of New York in a hurry. He wrote to the boss of his gang, Johnny Torrio, who had moved to Chicago. Torrio was looking for a ruthless hardman to help him build up a chain of gambling clubs and bars in "the windy city." Capone was just the man for the job.

At the beginning of the 20th century, Chicago was a sprawling city of three million inhabitants. It still had an untamed, frontier feel. Crowds of thirsty factory workers and cowboys from the surrounding prairies thronged its bars and nightclubs. It was a perfect place for an ambitious gangster to build an empire. But the heavy drinking and brawling that plagued Chicago and most other American cities had alarmed the government. In 1920, a group of concerned politicians succeeded in passing a law which they hoped would make the nation sober-up. This Prohibition Law made it illegal to make or sell alcohol. Overnight, Americans were expected to become teetotal.

It was a disaster from the start. Millions of citizens didn't think there was anything wrong with having a drink. So they turned to the only people who could help them: gangsters. Gangs smuggled whiskey into the country and brewed their own beer (which tasted revolting), selling it on at inflated prices. They were known as bootleggers. This odd expression originated in the southern states of America, where smugglers carried bottles of whiskey in the tops of their thigh-length leather boots. Bootlegging was big business. At the height of Prohibition, Chicago had 20,000 speakeasies and the gangsters were getting rich.

For four years, Capone worked his way up in the gang hierarchy. He had a shrewd business sense and, when this failed, he would use his fists to crush any opposition. Of course, with the vast profits that could be made from supplying alcohol, there was deadly competition between gangs. During the "beer wars" in Chicago, police estimated there were around 700 murders. It was one of the bloodiest periods in peacetime American history, and Al Capone was at the heart of it.

But, finally, his fame grew dangerous. The criminal control Capone exercised over Chicago was viewed as an insult to American values and the forces of law and order. In 1930, the Chicago Crime Commission declared him "Public Enemy Number One." They were out to crack Capone.

After years at the top, Capone had established an army of loyal gangsters, as well as corrupt police, judges and journalists, all dedicated to protecting him and his illegal businesses. Each month, he paid out millions of dollars in bribes. Never before had a criminal held so much power over a major American city. One independent journalist described how, during an interview, the gang boss was told that one of his gunmen was in police custody. Spitting with rage, Capone grabbed the telephone off his desk and called the judge who had ordered the arrest.

"I thought I told you to release that fellow," Capone screamed down the phone. The judge apologized. "Make sure it doesn't happen again," snapped Capone before hanging up.

Not only did this subservience make it difficult to charge Capone in the law courts, it also made it impossible to close any of his speakeasies or breweries. The policemen who were sent on raids were his informers and always warned him in advance. Capone even demanded squadrons of motorcycle cops to escort his beer trucks when he was worried other gangsters might try to hijack them. This corruption of the local authorities was perhaps Capone's most shocking achievement.

Faced with such a powerful enemy, the U.S. Department of Justice decided to attack on two fronts. They would select a team of honest men to raid Capone's distilleries and warehouses directly, hoping to starve him of the cash that he used to bribe city officials. Simultaneously, they would try to find a weakness in his legal position. Everyone knew that Capone was a big spender – he tipped waiters $100 bills and gave diamond belt buckles to his friends for birthday presents. But he didn't pay any taxes to the government. Elmer J. Irey, a brilliant senior agent for the U.S. tax office, was asked to investigate.

To lead the assault on the alcohol business, the Department of Justice chose a fresh-faced prohibition agent named Eliot Ness. He soon became known as "the man who couldn't be bought." Ness was born in Chicago in April 1903, and was only 26 when he was ordered to smash Capone. He was an ambitious, athletic and tough law graduate, who had studied criminology. Taking on America's most deadly gangster must have been a fascinating challenge for this star agent. He assembled a special squad of nine men he could trust, making a list of the skills he was looking for:

> *Single, no older than 30, with both the mental and physical stamina to work long hours and the courage and ability to use fists or gun and special investigative techniques.*

Ness knew full well that his mission was extremely dangerous. Capone was a cold-blooded killer and people who threatened him had a short life expectancy.

One story describes how the gangster discovered that three of his own men were cheating him. He invited them to an expensive restaurant, and was cracking jokes and smiling all night long. Suddenly, his bodyguards grabbed the guests and tied them to their chairs. Capone fetched a baseball bat. "The punishment for disloyalty," he snarled, "is death." And he beat the three terrified captives to a pulp.

But Ness was thrilled to be taking on "the Big Guy," as Capone was known around Chicago. He saw himself as a fearless Wild West sheriff and told his friends: "What the hell, I figured, nobody lives forever."

He named his chosen men "the Untouchables," to reinforce the message that they couldn't be bribed. By tapping into the phone calls of Capone's henchmen, the Untouchables soon discovered the locations of the hidden breweries and went to work.

Ness bought a powerful truck and welded a snow shovel to the radiator grill. In the back of the truck there were ladders with hooks on the end, so the Untouchables could climb over any barriers. At 5:00am, they gathered outside a downtown warehouse. The truck roared towards the heavy wooden gates and battered its way through. Ness and his team rushed in, impounding vehicles, arresting the men they found working there and smashing any distilling equipment with sledgehammers. After four or five raids like this, the Big Guy began to pay attention to the Untouchables.

Al Capone had always used two tactics to get what he wanted: bribery and force. Ness was promised $2,000 a week if he stopped raiding the factories. Even though the agent was only earning $3,000 a year, he threw the money in the face of the startled messenger who had delivered the offer.

Force came next. Ness was walking his girlfriend home one evening when he noticed a suspicious looking car. He took his girlfriend to her house, and then approached the car. When he was only a few steps away he noticed the steel of a gun barrel, glinting in the moonlight. This glimpse saved his life. He threw himself backwards and scrambled for his own vehicle. Gunshots smashed the windshield and peppered the driver's door. Ness grabbed his own gun, ready to fight it out, but the assassins had fled.

The Untouchables cost Capone millions of dollars, but they could never find enough proof to bring him to trial for prohibition crimes. Nevertheless, Eliot Ness seriously damaged the gangster's pride and taught him that he was vulnerable. On one occasion, the agent took great pleasure in parading 45 beer trucks he'd impounded from the beer raids in front of the Lexington Hotel, Capone's luxury headquarters. Capone was so furious he smashed two chairs and ran screaming from the room. But Ness still couldn't send the Big Guy to prison. For that, the Department of Justice turned to their accountants. Ness was such a daring, perhaps foolhardy, investigator, he tends to get all the credit for trapping Capone. But, in the end, the men who were most responsible for putting the gang boss behind bars were tax inspectors: Elmer Irey and Frank J. Wilson.

It was obvious to everyone that Al Capone was rich. If anyone had been in any doubt, his wealth was confirmed when he bought his own luxury hideaway in 1928 – Palm Island, just off the coast of Florida.

The island boasted a huge mansion, tropical gardens and a pier for his motor yacht. Capone even invited journalists to visit and take photos of the gardens. But, despite all his money, he had never paid any taxes. This was a federal crime – meaning it concerned the government, not the local state – and it was punishable by a fine or a prison sentence. Elmer Irey instructed one of his best men, Frank J. Wilson, a 43-year-old, successful federal agent, to prove that Al Capone had a huge income and was thus liable to pay tax.

Capone probably never guessed that, in America, even gangsters were supposed to pay their taxes. Most lawyers wouldn't advise a client to admit to any illegal earnings, in case it was used against them in a later prosecution. But, in 1927, the American supreme court passed the "Sullivan Decision": this stated that income raised from illegal activities *was* taxable.

Chicago tax agents had already pursued Al's elder brother, Ralph "Bottles" Capone, for unpaid taxes on his gambling earnings. Bottles had been sentenced to three years in jail. But the reason he was found guilty was because the agents had found a ledger – seized in a police raid on a gambling den – that linked his name to certain accounts. Bottles wasn't as smart as his younger brother. Al Capone never signed his name, didn't use a bank account and never bought anything except through an intermediary. Wilson knew he needed something in writing to show that

Capone was receiving an income. He began digging around for evidence.

In the meantime, Irey decided that if he had someone on the inside he might learn more about the complex business organization of Capone's gang. The man chosen was Mike Malone, a fearless agent who was fluent in Italian – a handy skill, since many of Capone's gang had Italian connections. By pretending to be a gangster from New York, he was offered a job as a croupier for the gang and started passing information back to Irey.

Another "plant," an agent using the code-name Graziano, soon joined Malone and overheard a conversation that turned out to be the beginning of the end for the Big Guy. Two gang members were mocking the tax investigation of their boss, and mentioned some ledger books that had been confiscated following a raid on one of Capone's bars.

"They've already got a book that could send the Big Guy to jail for five years, but they're too dumb to realize it," one of them said.

Graziano wasn't sure if the information was true, but he passed it along to Wilson just in case.

Wilson scoured through thousands of impounded documents until he came across a ledger from a gambling club. Two bookkeepers had made entries for hundreds of thousands of dollars owed to a "Mr. A. Capone." If Wilson could find these bookkeepers, he would have witnesses to testify that Capone was receiving an income from his gambling operations. But had they already been assassinated to protect the Big Guy?

Graziano bravely risked blowing his cover and his life by asking the gangster he'd overheard if the bookkeepers were still alive.

"Sure, they left town five years ago," came the cocky reply. Graziano could hardly believe his luck when the man told him their names.

Federal agents quickly traced the men to Miami and rural Illinois, and they agreed to give evidence against their former boss, as long as they received witness protection. This was a wise request. Within hours, Capone's police informants told him about the arrests and he had contracts for $50,000 put out on the bookkeepers' lives. The case against the Big Guy was getting stronger, but the gangster king still couldn't be underestimated. He was at his most dangerous when his back was against the wall.

Capone's first defensive tactic surprised everybody: cooperation. In the summer of 1930, he went to see Wilson, taking with him a tax expert. Capone said he wanted to pay his back taxes. The gangster admitted to earning $100,000 a year. Wilson demanded that this statement should be put down in writing and, foolishly, Capone agreed. The sly gangster thought he could get away with paying a few thousand dollars in fines. But Wilson knew that he spent more than $100,000 a year just on his own gambling habit and his tailored clothes.

Under pressure, Capone grudgingly admitted he received one sixth of the profits from his entire criminal organization – but no figures were provided. Now Wilson had a case he could take to court. The bookkeepers would decipher the ledger and show that the gambling business alone was making millions a year, and the Big Guy had confessed to receiving a sixth of all profits. The tax office calculated that Capone owed them $215,000, at least. They called him to trial.

Al Capone, the killer with ice-cold eyes, was getting nervous. For four years he had ruled Chicago without fear of arrest or prosecution. Now, his informers told him the government was ready to send him to jail. He decided to fight back. And, as before, he used his two most powerful tactics. One night, Frank Wilson received a desperate phone call from Mike Malone.

"Get out of your hotel. Scarface has hired five New York killers to rub you out."

The assassins were waiting for Wilson down in the street. But, at the last moment, Capone called the hit off. His advisors cautioned him against murdering federal officers. More bloodshed would only anger the Washington authorities further. Instead, Capone offered Elmer Irey $1,500,000 in a briefcase, in exchange for a full pardon. Irey was as good as the Untouchables: he refused.

Now Capone tried to cut a deal. He went to the Chicago District Attorney and said he'd plead guilty to the tax and prohibition charges in exchange for paying a huge fine and only serving a prison sentence of between two and three years. The prosecutor knew that if Capone pleaded not guilty, he could bribe the jury and be acquitted. As one lawman muttered, "Putting the Big Guy in jail is like catching a fish between your fingers." The District Attorney decided it was better to be sure of getting Capone into prison for a few years than risking his complete acquittal. He agreed to the deal.

Capone threw a wild going–away party and turned up on June 30, 1931 to be sentenced. But Judge Wilkerson had a surprise for him.

"There is no bargaining in the Federal Court," the judge announced. "I will decide on your sentence, and I alone."

Capone's deal with the District Attorney was torn up. Trembling with shock, the gangster changed his plea to "Not Guilty" and was called back to trial on October 6.

Capone's only chance now was to intimidate or bribe the jury that was going to hear his case. He spent thousands of dollars tracking down the jury members and making sure they wouldn't dare to convict him. But, on the morning of the trial, the cautious judge summoned the usher.

"Dismiss these jurors," ordered the judge. "Bring

me a jury from another court room."

Capone almost let out a sob as the new jury filed in. They were complete strangers to the gangster and his henchmen.

The trial lasted for 12 days. The prosecution produced witness after witness who had received money from Capone, so proving he had an income. Frank Wilson had been collecting the gangster's household bills. There were shirt-makers and gamblers, butchers and mechanics, all testifying that Capone had given them payment. Each small bill Wilson produced was proof that Capone had money coming in. Then the bookkeepers gave their evidence and Capone was doomed. It was clear he had received hundreds of thousands of dollars every year, but had paid no taxes on any of it. The Big Guy was found guilty.

On October 24, 1931, he came back for sentencing, expecting at most three to five years in jail, as a harsh punishment. In fact, he was given 11 years – more than double any previous penalty for tax evasion. As he left the court, he protested: "It was a blow below the belt, but what can you expect when the whole community is prejudiced against you? I never had a chance."

He was only 32 years old, and his reign was over. Eliot Ness escorted him to the prison train.

Capone served two years in the Atlanta Penitentiary and the rest of his sentence in the notorious Alcatraz Prison, in San Francisco Bay. This high-security jail was dreaded by even the most hardened criminals. Perched on a rocky island, it was surrounded by freezing, strong ocean currents, infested with sharks. But the dangers inside the prison walls were even worse.

The warden had imposed a regime based on the "Pennsylvania System," a prison experiment pioneered by members of the Quaker religion in the 1800s. Quakers considered prison to be a form of penance, rather than punishment (hence the word "penitentiary" for an American prison). Penance involves self-punishment and reflection, to pay for a transgression or sin. On Alcatraz, prisoners lived in silence, weren't allowed candy or cigarettes, and were left alone in their cells for much of their sentence. This way of life might work wonders for people who want a reclusive existence but, on Alcatraz, it had the effect of driving a lot of the prisoners insane.

Capone was finally released in 1939, physically withered and his mind irreparably damaged. The hard regime had worn him down, but there was another reason for his condition. For years, Capone had suffered from the ravages of syphilis, a degenerative disease he'd probably caught as a teenager. He was a broken man.

The Big Guy retired to Palm Island, where he lived quietly until his death on January 25, 1947. He died in his bed, unlike so many of his contemporaries.

Al Capone clambered his way to the top of the criminal world using mass murder and ruthlessness, never doubting his right to snatch what he wanted. Because of the mental decay doctors observed at Alcatraz, historians have suggested that he might have been a psychopath – a person with a damaged brain who experiences violent and antisocial impulses. Psychopaths often find it difficult to relate to other people, or show any emotion. They have difficulty deciding whether their actions are right or wrong, and think only about doing what's good for them.

Psychopath or not, Capone is still famous today because he was the first gangster to step out of the shadows. He gave interviews to national newspapers, and never turned down a chance to parade his wealth and power. For four years, he was the undisputed ruler of Chicago, in a breathtaking affront to law and order. It was Capone's arrogance and swagger that have ensured his lasting fame. For just a moment in history, people wondered if the gangsters were going to win.

Die young and famous

The men had been waiting in the woods for two days. They were hungry and stiff and covered in insect bites. Some of them wanted to call off the ambush and go back to town for a meal and a hot bath. Perhaps they were wasting their time, sitting out here in the Louisiana back country. But, as dawn came, they heard the growl of an engine in the distance. Quickly, they checked their high-power rifles and positioned themselves in a line, like a firing squad overlooking the road. A few minutes later, a Ford saloon skidded around the corner and slowed down to inspect a pick-up truck that had been parked at the side of the track: a decoy to make the Ford driver stop for a look. Ted Hinton, a Texan police deputy, was nearest to the Ford. He could see the young man behind the steering wheel, the pretty girl next to him eating a sandwich.

"This is him," he whispered to the other five hunters, hidden in the roadside bushes. There was no warning. The men took aim and opened fire.

It was May 23, 1934. Bonnie and Clyde were ripped to pieces as over 100 bullets smashed into the side of their car. Nothing could have survived this firepower. Their Ford span out of control and slammed into a ditch.

Ted Hinton ran down to the wreck and pulled the passenger door open. Bonnie's blood-splattered body fell into his arms. He noticed the scent of her perfume. The detective must have remembered the first time he'd seen her, five years earlier when she'd served him coffee in a Dallas diner. The young waitress had told him of her ambition to be an actress or singer. She wanted everyone to know her name. She wanted to be famous.

Bonnie Parker was born in 1910, in the small farming town of Rowena, Texas. But, after the death of her father, the family moved to a tough suburb of Dallas. Bonnie was devoted to her mother, who worked hard to give her a good childhood, even though money was tight. At school she was an excellent pupil, winning prizes for her writing and spelling. She was confident and pretty, and she knew how to look after herself. If any of the school children made fun of her or her friends, Bonnie wasn't scared to fight them with her fists.

At 16, Bonnie married her high-school sweetheart, Roy Thornton. She was a gifted, popular girl, but she had bad taste in men. After the wedding, Thornton went missing for several months, and he offered no explanation upon his return. This soon became a habit.

Bonnie was lonely and she needed money, so she took a job as a waitress. She enjoyed the work, and the customers found her cheerful and attractive. Among them was Ted Hinton, who remembered her as "a girl who could turn heads." Perhaps the job at the diner gave her a new confidence. The next time Thornton came home, she told him she didn't love him and asked him to move out.

Two months later, her husband was convicted of robbery and sentenced to five years in jail. During the absences from Bonnie, he'd been breaking into banks. Even though she didn't love him, Bonnie refused to divorce Thornton: "That would be like a betrayal," she told her mother.

So she was still his wife on the day she died. Bonnie's tiny physique – she was only four feet ten inches tall – belied an enormous loyalty to her family and those she loved. It was this loyalty that would get her killed.

Clyde Barrow was born into a life of grinding, rural poverty in the plains around Dallas, Texas, in 1909. He worked in the fields as soon as he could walk. His family sometimes went without food, and their clothes were torn and tattered. Clyde hated school and, instead of attending classes, he wandered the local countryside. He was often neglected and alone, inventing games to keep himself entertained. But there was an ugly side to some of these games. His first brush with the police came after local farmers complained they'd seen a young boy torturing animals. Clyde had broken the wing of a bird and then watched, fascinated, as the terrified animal attempted to fly away.

When Clyde was 12, his family moved to the suburbs of West Dallas, to a tough area known as "the Bog." Clyde began stealing cars and breaking into houses. By the time he was 21, he was holding-up grocery stores and the police were on the lookout for him.

One evening he dropped in on a friend, who'd broken her arm in an ice-skating accident.

"I've come to cheer you up," he told her. "But what's all that noise in the kitchen?"

"My friend Bonnie Parker's helping with the chores. Go and say hello."

Clyde stepped into the kitchen. Bonnie was making some hot chocolate at the stove. They stared at each other for a moment, and that was enough: they were in love.

For three months they were inseparable. Then Clyde was arrested and sent to jail. Bonnie wrote to him:

Please don't ever do anything to get locked up again... I want you to be a man, honey, and not a thug... we are young and should be happy like other boys and girls instead of being like we are...

But it was too late to change Clyde Barrow. Bonnie was hopelessly in love with a man who had never known adult guidance or discipline as a child. Clyde barely knew right from wrong. Crime gave him easy money and a sense of power. He would do anything to escape the poverty of his childhood – no matter what the risk.

Clyde ignored her letter and asked Bonnie to smuggle a revolver into his prison cell. Ever loyal, she did as he asked, hoping that once he was free they could run away somewhere and start a new life. He broke out of jail, but a week later he was recaptured and sent to a much tougher prison, the Huntsville Penitentiary, known as "the Walls."

The Texan prison system was brutal. Clyde was moved to a prison farm where he had to pick cotton and build roads, in the blazing summer heat or chilly winter wind. Guards whipped the prisoners with a long leather strap called "the bat," and they were under orders to "shoot to kill" anyone attempting to escape. Knife-fights and beatings were common between the inmates. Shocked by the violence of prison life, Clyde developed an intense hatred for authority and any officer of the law. In fact, he was so desperate to get a transfer from the prison farm, he asked a fellow convict to hack off two of his toes with an axe. But the prison governor, Lee Simmons, was a tough man. He was unimpressed with Clyde's injuries and refused to move him. Simmons would be one of the men responsible for Clyde's bloody death only two years later.

Prison did little to reform Clyde Barrow. As soon as he got parole, he picked up Bonnie and set out to rob a grocery store.

But their first crime together went badly wrong. Halfway through the attempted robbery, the police arrived.

"Run for the car!" Clyde screamed.

But their getaway car was stuck in heavy mud. So they set off on foot across open fields, with the police in pursuit.

"I can see some horses up ahead," said Clyde. "We can ride them to safety."

The horses were, in fact, mules. Even so, the Barrow gang (Bonnie, Clyde and a new recruit named Ralph Fults) rolled around in the mud chasing after the animals. When they finally caught three of them, the mules were in no mood to be ridden anywhere. With the police closing in, the gang sat atop their stationary mounts, desperately urging them to gallop away. At last, they dismounted and made a run for it. Bonnie and Ralph were arrested, but Clyde escaped. This robbery was a taste of things to come: Clyde was a bungler and a useless gang leader.

Bonnie was a model prisoner while she awaited trial for the grocery robbery. Her smile and fresh face made a good impression on the jury. On June 17, 1932, she was released, and went straight back to Clyde. They had survived the failed robbery and mule getaway unscathed. But Clyde Barrow's next moment of panic was to have more deadly consequences for their future.

For two years after his release from prison, Clyde roamed the back roads of Texas and its border states, forcing Bonnie to eat and sleep in the back of stolen cars. Because she loved him, she stayed with him. Also, she enjoyed the thrill of reading her name in the papers and rapidly becoming a household name. It's a good thing Bonnie wasn't in it for the money. The gang didn't make any. In two years they stole only a few thousand dollars. Most of their crimes were robberies from gas stations and grocery shops – sometimes, they were stealing hamburgers and milkshakes because they were so hungry.

New criminals would join the gang for a few weeks, thinking they'd soon get rich, but then desert once they realized how incompetent a leader Clyde was. On one occasion, he burst into a small country bank to find only one old man sitting in the corner of the room. The bank had closed for business four days earlier. But this was how Bonnie and Clyde lived. They had started their crime spree and they didn't know how to stop it.

Duke Ellis was playing his guitar at a country dance in Springtown, Oklahoma, when he noticed a dark car pull up next to the dancing platform with three men inside. It was a humid, summer evening in August 1932, and Ellis watched the strangers taking swigs from a whiskey bottle. One man clambered out and strolled over to join the dance – he was never identified. Clyde Barrow and a new gang member, Raymond Hamilton, remained in the car.

Ellis wasn't the only one who'd noticed the visitors.

"Let's take a look," the local sheriff told his deputy.

But, as the lawmen walked over to investigate, there was a sudden explosion of gunfire. The car accelerated away, only to crash into a ditch. Barrow and Hamilton jumped out and started shooting into the terrified crowd, before running into the darkness and hijacking a passing motorist.

The deputy was shot through the heart and died instantly, and the sheriff was seriously wounded. This cowardly murder of a policeman could have been avoided if Clyde had been cool-headed enough to disarm the officers – neither policeman had drawn a gun. But Clyde had panicked once again.

"You've killed a cop?" Bonnie asked him in disbelief. But her loyalty was unshakeable. Even though she'd had nothing to do with the shooting, she didn't consider leaving him. "So, what do we do now?" she cried.

"Keep driving," answered Clyde, "just keep driving from now till they get us."

Clyde had no grand plan or brilliant idea that would allow the gang to retire. He just wanted to live on the road, outside the law, as long as he could. Bonnie still hoped there was a chance for them to get away from Texas and settle down somewhere. But with the arrival of Clyde's criminal brother, Buck, their problems were about to get worse.

Buck was out on parole and had promised his law-abiding wife, Blanche, that he was finished with crime. Blanche had already had a few surprises with her new husband. When she married him, she had no idea he was in fact an escaped convict. She'd finally managed to persuade him to turn himself in and waited patiently for him to get his parole. On his release, he told her he only wanted to see his brother for a few days before taking up an honest life, perhaps working as a farmer. The two couples rented an apartment in Joplin, Missouri, along with 17-year-old gang member, W.D. Jones. The Barrow brothers played cards and chatted while their wives cooked and read magazines. But the other residents in the apartment building grew suspicious of the new tenants. They'd seen Jones lifting something out of his car that looked like it might have been a gun wrapped in a blanket.

One afternoon, the police arrived. The first officer to approach the block was shot down by Clyde Barrow with a sawn-off shotgun.

"Bonnie!" he screamed, "the law's outside."

Bonnie, still wearing her slippers and a negligee, responded by spraying the police with machine-gun rounds. Clyde shot another policeman in the arm and then rushed for his car. Whether Blanche liked it or not, she and her husband were in the gang now. They ran down to the waiting car, jumped in and drove away.

"I'm shot," moaned Clyde.

There was blood oozing from a hole in his chest. Bonnie leaned across and dug around in the open wound with a hatpin until she found the bullet. It was a ricochet bullet (meaning it had bounced off another object before hitting Clyde), so most of its destructive power had been lost. It had only broken his skin. Clyde's luck was holding – but for how much longer?

The gunfight at Joplin received national newspaper coverage. Two policemen had been murdered and the killers had escaped. But, in their flight, the gang had left plenty of evidence for the police to identify them. Blanche had left behind her handbag, with Buck's name on their wedding certificate inside. Bonnie had dropped a pile of magazine stories and a poem she was writing, *The Story of Suicide Sal*, describing the harsh life of a gangster's moll. The local press found out about the poem and pricked up their ears. When they discovered two rolls of undeveloped camera film, they went into a frenzy.

Bonnie, Clyde and Jones had been fooling around with a camera, striking poses with their fearsome collection of weapons. There was a shot of Bonnie holding a shotgun pointed at Clyde. The gun was huge in her tiny hands. And there was another picture, of a beautiful Bonnie holding a revolver and smoking a cigar. It was a defiant image, a "come and get me" challenge to the police. The fact that Bonnie didn't smoke and was only playing with the cigar didn't interfere with her new reputation as a "cigar-smoking moll." The photograph was published at once, in the *Joplin Globe* newspaper. It was the birth of the Bonnie and Clyde myth. And it allowed the police to identify the gang members. Their faces were plastered across "Wanted" posters all over the southern states of America. Bonnie and Clyde were becoming too famous for their own good.

It was late July, 1933, and employees at the Red Crown Motel in Platte City, Missouri, were growing concerned about a group of people who had arrived in the middle of the night and rented two apartments. Only one woman, Blanche, ventured out to collect their food and pay the bills. For some reason, the other guests never left their rooms. The owner of the motel, Emmett Breen, decided to call the police.

Taking no chances, the police arrived with a bulletproof car and steel body shields they could stand behind. But the Barrow gang had raided a National Guard weapons store a month earlier and were equipped with high-powered rifles. As soon as the police called out a warning, Clyde fired a fusillade from his Browning automatic rifle. The bullets tore through the metal shields and into the police officers. They even penetrated the bulletproof car and wounded the driver. Then the gang jumped into their own car and escaped into the night.

This time, they hadn't been so lucky. Buck had been shot in the head and was lapsing in and out of consciousness. Blanche had been blinded by a glass window exploding next to her eyes and was bleeding heavily. After driving through the night and most of the next day, the bullet-pocked car arrived at the Dexfield Park picnic ground near Des Moines, Iowa. Clyde knew they had to make camp and treat the injured, but it was dangerous to stop in a public area. He decided to take the risk.

The gang was cooking breakfast when the police moved in. A local farmer had discovered the wounded visitors in the park and the police had gathered as many riflemen as possible to surround the area.

It was a chaotic shoot-out. Clyde was hit in the arm as he tried to get the car started, Bonnie was sprayed with shotgun pellets and Jones was shot in the head. Buck, already badly wounded, was shot several times in the back and head – but kept firing at the police despite his injuries. Under this cover, Bonnie, Clyde and Jones managed to scramble into the woods and escape across a river. Buck died in the hospital five days after the gunfight. Blanche was sent to jail for ten years.

Perhaps it was then that Bonnie realized there was no way out for them, except death. The two gangster lovers began to make secret visits to their families in Dallas. It was at one of these meetings that Bonnie gave her mother a copy of another poem she'd written: *The Story of Bonnie and Clyde*. This was a romantic depiction of their life together as gangsters, fighting the police who would, she knew, eventually destroy them.

"When we're gone," she begged her mother, "don't let them say cruel things about us."

On the other side of town, a specially selected group of men were preparing to go after the gang. Ted Hinton was 29 and had been raised in the Bog, the same Dallas suburb where the Barrow boys had grown up. But Hinton had resisted the lure of gangster life and joined the police force. He knew Bonnie and Clyde and their families by sight, and he'd been ordered to bring them in.

Bob Alcorn was another Dallas policeman on the team, chosen because of his skill with a rifle. He was a crack shot.

Joining these two deputies was a former Texas Ranger, Frank Hamer. Prison governor Lee Simmons had recruited him after Barrow organized a prison break at the Walls to free one of his gang, along with two other inmates. A guard died in the escape shoot-out. Simmons had promised the guard's family he would capture the murderer. Hamer, now in his fifties, was a famous "man-tracker." As a boy he'd spent weeks living alone in the forest, learning tracking and hunting skills. Like Alcorn, he was a dead shot. He enlisted his own assistant, Manny Gault.

Their plan was to exploit the gang's chief weakness: their longing to see their families. Bonnie and Clyde weren't loners. They'd always enjoyed the company of their parents and siblings. Though they were careful about the planning and secrecy of their clandestine visits, perhaps one of the other gang members would be less cautious. The hunters decided to search the Louisiana countryside around the home of the latest member of the Barrow gang, 21-year-old Henry Methvin, one of the men Clyde had freed from prison. They didn't have long to wait.

"They've been staying at old man Methvin's place," an informer told them.

The policemen set up an ambush on the road that led to the Methvin cabin. They were joined by the county sheriff, Henderson Jordan, and his deputy, Prentis Oakley.

The six men soon spotted a truck approaching. It was Irvin Methvin, Henry's father. The policemen handcuffed him to the trunk of a tree and moved his truck off the road to work as a decoy. And then they waited.

It was the end of the road for the Barrow gang.

Bonnie and Clyde died a violent death. Whether they were reckless young lovers who refused to bow down to authority, or clumsy, ruthless killers, they weren't given the chance to make their case in a courtroom. In two years they had killed 12 people, including five policemen. The men who shot them claimed that it was too dangerous to give any warning. Clyde had already shot his way out of every attempted arrest. They lived and died by the gun.

On the way to the furniture store that doubled as an undertakers in the small town of Arcadia, Louisiana, crowds of people blocked the road to gawp at the shattered car and the corpses it contained. They tried to snatch pieces of Bonnie's dress, bits of glass from the shattered windshield, strands of Clyde's hair. The newspapers had been running stories about the pair for months, and the daring photos from the Joplin raid had turned them into criminal celebrities. Simmons arrived and congratulated the bewildered detectives in front of cheering crowds.

Ten thousand people flocked to Arcadia, to stare at Bonnie's broken body, and that of her lover. Bonnie Parker got her wish. She was one of the most famous women in America – famous for being a gangster.

Desert dreamer

Hollywood has always been a place for dreamers. The lure of movie stardom draws thousands of hopeful actors to the sun-drenched Los Angeles suburb every year. Most of them end up flipping burgers or pumping gas for a few months, while chasing directors for auditions and pestering the movie studios for an interview. They soon learn L.A. is a tough town, and making a name for yourself there is even tougher. Only a few stick it out to see their dreams come true. Some accomplish it through hard work and a little luck. Others are more savage, reasoning that, in a city full of sharks, they'll only succeed through ruthless determination. They don't let anyone get in their way.

Benjamin Siegel arrived in Los Angeles in the summer of 1935. He drove a brand-new, top of the range Cadillac, wore silk shirts and Italian suits, and rented a mansion with 35 rooms. Siegel had a friend in town, the movie actor, George Raft. He started going to film-studio parties with Raft, introducing himself to the stars and starlets as a sportsman. Suave, six feet tall and chatty, Siegel soon became a popular addition to the Hollywood society set. He sipped martinis with Clark Gable, Cary Grant and Jean Harlow, and was a daily visitor to Raft's luxurious home, where he often took a dip in the pool. He lived the life of a Hollywood playboy, and made plans to build his own white-brick mansion in the heart of Beverly Hills.

But, like so many others in "Tinseltown," Siegel was putting on an act. His friend Raft was famous for playing gangsters. Movie critics said his acting was so realistic, you could almost believe Raft *was* a gangster. It was as though he'd studied them at close quarters. And so he had. One of the most dangerous gangsters in the country liked to swim in his pool.

Ben Siegel was better known as "Bugsy." This was a gangster expression for someone who was aggressive, fearless in a fight, and perhaps a little crazy. For ten years, Bugsy and his gang had terrorized

New York with the violence that earned him his nickname. He worked in partnership with another gangster, Meyer Lansky, who made all the tactical decisions for the gang. Bugsy acted as the enforcer, meting out punishments and protecting the gang's empire. Where Lansky used guile and diplomacy, Bugsy used bullets to get what he wanted. He was forceful and dynamic, but it was only through his association with Lansky that Bugsy had risen so high in the criminal elite. Siegel was too impulsive, reckless and violent for his own good – and it had earned him a period in exile.

After a high-profile, bloody shooting in 1934, the New York gang leaders had asked "the Bug" to leave town for a while. He was getting too much police attention for their liking. So he boarded a train to Los Angeles, took over the running of the west coast gangs and began making plans for his future. Like everyone else in Hollywood, Bugsy had a dream, and he wasn't going to let anybody stand in its way.

The gangster had two ambitions in life: to get rich, and to use this fortune to be accepted by high society. He was tired of the lawless life, the constant threat of arrest from the police, and the dreaded risk of being taken on "a one-way drive" by rival crooks. Bugsy knew all too well what happened on one of those. The victim usually ended up on the bottom of a lake, tied to a lump of concrete.

Bugsy had already made a lot of money from his

criminal operations, but he had an expensive lifestyle to support. He wanted more than the gangs were giving him. And there were advantages to earning his fortune by honest means. It would keep him out of prison and put him in good stead with his "respectable" friends. So, as soon as he reached California, he began building a new life. He threatened journalists with beatings if they made any reference to his criminal past, he avoided the company of other gangsters, and he reacted furiously if anyone dared to call him "Bugsy" to his face. He sent his two young daughters to an expensive riding school and joined the local country club. Bugsy would use his gangster money and connections when it suited him, but all the while he was thinking of schemes that would help him escape his old life of crime. Some of those schemes were madcap, to say the least.

Within a few months of settling in Los Angeles, he heard of an idea that could defy the strict, Californian anti-gambling laws, and help him become a millionaire. Prohibition had been overturned, and the rich pickings from illegally importing liquor on the high seas from Canada and Mexico had vanished overnight. This left a lot of boats and their captains with no income. One of these "booze pirates" – and a man who really did steal alcohol from other ships – was named Tony Cornero. He wanted to fit out a steamship, the *Rex*, with gaming tables and one-armed bandits, and moor it a few miles out to sea, off the coast of Los Angeles. Once the boat was in international waters, it would be exempt from the ban on gambling – which, unlike bootlegging, was still illegal. Cornero approached Bugsy, who was a hopeless gambler himself, and persuaded him to invest thousands of dollars in the scheme.

The boat anchored 5km (3 miles) offshore and Cornero ferried eager customers out to the card tables in a fleet of water taxis. But 5km wasn't far enough; detectives raided the ship, claiming it was still within Californian waters. So Cornero set sail again, this time dropping anchor 19km (12 miles) out to sea. Now the police lost interest. But so did the gamblers. Twelve miles in a motorboat was quite a journey, and seasickness destroyed Bugsy's first hope of making a million.

For his next "get-rich-quick" scheme, Bugsy teamed up with another Hollywood dreamer – Countess Dorothy di Frasso. The countess was an eccentric and beautiful millionairess who had fallen for Bugsy's animal charms. She was well-connected in Hollywood society, and Siegel used her shamelessly to get introductions to all the people he considered important. For months, he escorted her to fashionable parties and courted her friends. The Count di Frasso was far away, living in the family villa in Venice, but the countess preferred the bright lights of Los Angeles. She was a gambler like Bugsy, and she loved plotting high-risk wheezes.

Her latest idea was no exception. On a trip to New York, the countess had bought a treasure map, and she invited Bugsy to lead an expedition to find the buried booty. Bugsy, di Frasso and a motley crew of Hollywood drinkers and hired guns set sail towards the equator on a chartered schooner, the *Metha Nelson*. By the time they were off the coast of Mexico, Bugsy had mustered the crew on deck and revealed their secret mission. They were bound for Cocos Island, a mountainous, bug-infested rock that was the property of Costa Rica. A treasure had been hidden there long ago, by the crew of an English ship, the *Mary Deere*, and if the stories Di Frasso had heard were true, it might be worth as much as $90,000,000 in the form of gold and jewels.

The tough gangsters that Bugsy had recruited to protect the ship from pirates couldn't believe what they were hearing. Had the Bug lost his mind? How could he be taken in by these fairy tales? But nobody wanted to be the one to tell him he was gullible or crazy, so the voyage continued.

The *Metha Nelson* pushed out into the open Pacific. Soon the dark shape of their treasure island reared up on the horizon. The ship anchored and a party was sent ashore. Except for hordes of rats, wild pigs and thousands of snakes, the treasure-hunters were alone. They pitched tents and the next morning began their work.

For ten days they dug and dynamited their way around the barren island. They were drenched by tropical rains, burned by the sun and ravaged by biting insects. On the eleventh day, Bugsy ordered them back to the ship. He was beaten. There was no gold, no jewels, nothing but dirt. The Bug realized he'd lost another high-risk bet. As soon as they reached the mainland, he flew back to Los Angeles in a sulk, leaving the countess and the crew to sail back alone, struggling through storms and fierce arguments over their failed mission.

Years later, the FBI (the Federal Bureau of Investigation, America's elite squad of investigators based in Washington) suggested that the voyage in the *Metha Nelson* had been nothing more than a cover story for Bugsy to meet Mexican drug lords. While the ship was anchored, he could have courted local gangsters and discussed plans for smuggling drugs into California. But this cunning idea probably never occurred to Siegel. If the treasure hunt had been a decoy, it seems unlikely that he'd have spent ten days digging pointlessly for a fantasy treasure. You might also think that the last thing he'd get involved in would be another of the countess's lunatic schemes. But that is precisely what he did...

Dorothy di Frasso had met two chemists who'd been working on a new explosive, named "Atomite." At a bizarre demonstration in the desert, Bugsy and di Frasso watched as a tiny amount of Atomite was detonated, leaving a huge crater in the sand. In the 1930s, this kind of explosive power was revolutionary. The countess and the Bug were so impressed, they agreed to invest thousands of dollars in the invention, in return for a share of its future profits. Di Frasso even wrote to her husband to tell him of her discovery, and he was sure that the Prime Minister of Italy, Benito Mussolini, would be interested in the new explosive. Mussolini's government was preparing the country for war and investing heavily in its armed forces.

A startled Bugsy found himself on a boat sailing for Rome, to give Mussolini a demonstration of Atomite's awesome power. But, while at sea, Bugsy began to suspect that the two chemists had already sold their explosive formula to another nation. The scientists seemed shifty and uncomfortable about the visit to Italy. Sure enough, when they arrived in Rome and Mussolini eagerly arranged a demonstration, Atomite had lost its punch. The powder that the chemists provided wouldn't even give off a few sparks.

Bugsy never found out what the problem was, but the damage was done. Mussolini was furious. As a punishment he confiscated the di Frasso villa, installing some of his fascist friends there when they came to visit Venice. Years later, Bugsy claimed that he had met Hermann Goering and Joseph Goebbels at the villa and almost lost his temper with them. Bugsy was Jewish, and the Nazi generals were both vicious anti-Semites. Before he could reach for his gun, the countess begged him not to harm them, as she was worried about the consequences for her Italian relatives. Bugsy reluctantly backed down.

The last of the countess's schemes concerned sharks – not the Hollywood variety, but the ones swimming in the ocean. It was early 1941 and, although America hadn't joined the Second World War, the country was suffering shortages of certain foods and medicines. Vitamin supplements were particularly hard to find in the shops.

"Shark livers are full of vitamin A," the countess told Bugsy one night, in a hushed voice. "If we could catch a few thousand sharks and extract the vitamins, we'd make a killing."

At first, Siegel thought this was a crazy idea, even by the countess's standards, but she soon talked him into it. They chartered a fishing boat and sent it trawling around the Pacific waters between Los Angeles and southern Mexico. The sharks must have seen them coming though, because after several months of raising empty nets, the venture was scrapped with huge losses. After this, Siegel swore he wouldn't listen to any more of di Frasso's eccentric investment ideas.

But by now the Bug had his own plan for making a fortune. He'd been busy in Los Angeles over the years, running a lucrative illegal radio service for the New York gang leaders. This broadcast the national horse-racing results in real-time, and no bookmaker could afford to be without it. Bugsy had assembled an efficient gang of his own, to give him independence from Meyer Lansky, and had been schmoozing with high society. Now he was ready for the biggest gamble of his whole gangster career: Bugsy was going to open a casino in the desert.

He visualized a high-class resort town of luxury casinos, shops and leisure facilities, all laid out around a sun-baked town called Las Vegas. When Bugsy arrived on the West coast, Las Vegas consisted of a few rundown bars and gambling halls for the miners and soldiers who lived out in the desert. It was a depressing place.

Gambling was allowed there because the state of Nevada had softened their laws to raise badly needed revenue. Reno, in the north of the state, had grown into a bustling town of casinos and hotels. But Las Vegas was in the south, in the middle of a scorching desert. It was about as hospitable as the surface of the moon. Arid, treeless and eroded by occasional sandstorms, it was horribly hot. Death Valley was only a few miles to the north of the city. On one oven-hot day when a flock of birds was flying over this cauldron, they dropped out of the sky, dead from heat exhaustion.

Everyone assumed Las Vegas had too harsh a terrain and climate to grow into a large resort. Why would tourists want to journey into such a desert to go gambling? But Bugsy decided to bet everything he had on turning Las Vegas into the biggest gambling resort in America.

In the summer of 1945, Bugsy bought a 30-acre plot of land on the outskirts of the town. It was a barren site, home only to coyotes and rattlesnakes. But here, Bugsy was going to build the most extravagant hotel in the West: the *Flamingo*.

"People will drive hundreds of miles just to see it," he told his incredulous gangster partners. "I want the walls and foundations to be twice as thick as other hotels. The *Flamingo's* going to last forever. Las Vegas will become famous all over the world as a luxury gambling town, and it's going to make us all rich."

He demanded $1,000,000 of funding from the gang leaders back in New York, and made fantastic promises about the financial returns they could expect as soon as the hotel opened. True to his word, no expense was spared in the construction of the *Flamingo*. Bugsy used all his gangster connections to get around the strict wartime controls on the supply of building materials and, when he couldn't find what he wanted in the U.S., he imported it on the black market. Marble, rare woods and fine carpets were trucked in, along with copper, tiles and expensive air-conditioning equipment. Skilled workmen were imported too: builders and craftsmen had to be flown in from other West coast cities.

Everything cost twice as much as it would have in Los Angeles. The hotel leaked money, and some of the suppliers took advantage of Bugsy's haphazard accounting. The palm trees that were brought in from Los Angeles to line the approach roads to the casino went missing each night, and Bugsy would have to buy more the next morning. Some crooks joked that the Bug was buying the same tree five times over.

Opening night was scheduled for December 26, 1946, and it was vital that it was a success. Bugsy was looking forward to reaping the rewards of all his careful networking in Hollywood. But, to guarantee good newspaper coverage of the *Flamingo* opening, he had to convince the movie stars to venture out from their Los Angeles mansions. So Bugsy hired two planes to fly them to the desert resort, paid thousands of dollars in magazine advertizing and publicity fees, and pressured George Raft to round up as many stars and starlets as possible. Despite some of the building work being behind schedule, everything was ready for the launch party. Siegel changed into a white tuxedo and waited for his dream to come true.

But, in true Bugsy-style, it was a disaster.

Loyal George Raft had driven out to his friend's casino in a sports car, but he was the only movie star who showed up. The chartered planes were stranded in thick fog at Los Angeles airport, and they were empty anyway. After hearing stories that Bugsy had been a gangster, the studio agents and bosses had told their actors not to associate with him. (This was before the days when Las Vegas was the place to be seen.) The stars stayed away, and so did everyone else. On opening night there were more employees than customers in the casino. The building itself had all kinds of teething problems and nothing seemed to work properly. Worse than this, some of the dealers turned out to be crooks, and the *Flamingo* became the first casino in history to lose money. It took Bugsy a few days to find out who was responsible and, in the meantime, the New York bosses were fuming about their failed investment. It was a terrible weekend for everyone: poor Raft managed to lose $60,000 at the card tables.

The *Flamingo* limped along for three weeks, losing money and failing to attract any new customers, until Bugsy accepted the inevitable and closed it down.

Still, Siegel wasn't ready to give up on his dream. He waited until all the construction work was properly finished, begged his old friend Meyer Lansky to raise some more money from the gangs, and reopened in the spring. This time, he would be ruthless in making the *Flamingo* a success. Siegel worked around the clock to make sure every detail was right. He booked top-class singers and comedians to give concerts, he increased the one-armed bandit jackpots, and he charmed journalists and editors to write reviews and features about his "card palace" in the desert.

Slowly, his hard work began to get results. The *Flamingo* was, at last, drawing in the crowds. If Bugsy could hold out until the lucrative summer season, his dream might yet come true.

Unfortunately, Bugsy was broke and his casino still wasn't making any money. If he couldn't meet his running costs, he'd never survive until the summer. The New York gangsters were already furious with his failed promises and refused to loan him any more cash. In desperation, Bugsy made a ruthless decision. The horse-race wire service he'd been operating was a real money-spinner. Bugsy received the rents from every Californian betting shop, took a cut and passed the rest to the New York gangs. Faced with his beloved *Flamingo* having to close once again, he doubled his cut. The gangsters reacted predictably, threatening Bugsy with a one-way ride if he didn't hand over the money. But Siegel was tough. He refused to back down.

With this cash injection, the *Flamingo* struggled on towards the summer. The hotel rooms were filling up and the tables were busy. Bugsy, exhausted after months of managing the casino, slipped back to Los Angeles to visit friends and relax for a few days.

On the evening of June 20, 1947, he was lounging on a sofa at a girlfriend's Beverly Hills house, talking with a friend about his plans for the future. Nine shots rang out in the night air. Bugsy slumped forward, his handsome face blown apart by the bullets from a powerful army rifle.

Gangland killings are notoriously hard to solve.

The killers are often professional assassins, with no link to the victim or the town where the murder takes place. Because of the reluctance of criminals to talk to the police, few of the gangster's friends came forward with evidence.

No one was ever arrested or charged with Siegel's murder, although there was no shortage of suspects. Bugsy had bullied, lied to and cheated hundreds of people in his years in California. In the last few months of his life, he had risked everything to keep the *Flamingo* running.

Within a few years of Bugsy's death, Las Vegas became the gambling sensation he had hoped for. The *Flamingo* was a star among the other casinos — and the town is still one of the most popular resorts on the planet today. But Bugsy Siegel, Hollywood dreamer, wasn't there to see it.

Betrayed by the lady in red

It had been a long, hot summer in Chicago, Illinois. After being cooped up all day in his baking apartment, John Dillinger was desperate for the air-conditioned cool of a movie house. He called out to his girlfriend, Polly, and the woman they were staying with, Anna Sage: "Ladies, better get ready to go out. There's a Clark Gable movie I want to see. He plays a killer who has to go to the electric chair."

A few months earlier, Dillinger would never have

dared to walk the city streets in daylight. He was a gangster, the "Most Wanted" man in America. There were police posters with his prison mug shots everywhere, offering $15,000 for his capture. But now the plastic surgery scars on his face and fingertips were healed, he'd grown a moustache and dyed his hair. Dillinger had a new face and a new name: Jimmy Lawrence. All he needed was the haul from one last job, a mail train robbery he'd been carefully planning, and he'd have enough money to leave the country for good. Mexico beckoned. America was getting too dangerous for him. He was running out of people he could trust.

"Wait for me one minute," called Sage, "I have to run down to the delicatessen to buy something."

"Don't be too long," Dillinger shouted.

On her way back, Sage stopped to make a phone call to Melvin Purvis, FBI agent. "He's here," she whispered. "We're leaving in five minutes."

It was July 22, 1934, and the incredible career of John Herbert Dillinger was almost at its end.

Dillinger was born in 1903, in Indianapolis, Indiana. His early life was unremarkable except for his prowess on the baseball field. Dillinger was a star athlete, handsome and lithe. But his performance in the classroom was less spectacular. He played truant, formed a gang called "The Dirty Dozen," and drifted in and out of trouble with the local police. His relations with his father were strained, but he was devoted to his stepmother, and she to him. After leaving school and doing a six-month stint in the navy, which he hated, he returned to Mooresville, Indiana, where his family had settled. There, he married 16-year-old Beryl Hovias, found a job and was trying to build a life for himself and his young wife when he fell in with an ex-convict, Ed Singleton, the umpire for Dillinger's baseball team.

One evening, the two men were sitting up drinking "moonshine" and telling each other stories.

"Hey," said Singleton suddenly, "you know the grocer, Frank Morgan?"

"Of course I do," answered Dillinger. "What about him?"

"Tonight he'll be walking home with the week's takings from his shop. Alone."

"Is that right?" said Dillinger, trying to sound tough in front of the older man.

"We could take that money for ourselves," whispered Singleton with a sly grin. "Are you with me?"

Dillinger was impressed by Singleton and agreed to help him in the robbery. Armed with a pistol and a bolt wrapped in a handkerchief, Dillinger surprised Morgan while Singleton waited with the getaway car. But Morgan fought back. When his gun went off by accident, Dillinger panicked and ran away.

Mooresville was a small town and Morgan recognized his attackers. The next morning, the sheriff arrived with an arrest warrant. Dillinger's father was an upright citizen. He persuaded his son to turn himself in. The local judge and the sheriff promised that the sentence would be lenient if he pleaded guilty. John Dillinger was 21 years old. He loved his wife and he didn't want this one drunken incident to ruin the rest of his life. So, he decided to take his father's advice and accept his punishment. In court, Dillinger didn't ask for a lawyer and he pleaded guilty to all charges.

The judge sentenced him to ten years in jail. His partner in the crime hired a lawyer. Despite his criminal record, Singleton only spent two years behind bars. Dillinger served nine years before he was paroled. In that time he made friends with the most vicious and violent bank robbers in the midwest, his wife divorced him and his beloved stepmother died before he could reach her bedside. Those long years in jail scarred him forever. In a letter to his father, written in his prison cell, he declared:

I know I have been a big disappointment to you but I guess I did too much time in jail... I went in a carefree boy, I came out bitter toward everything.

As soon as he was released, Dillinger set out to rob banks and attack the system that had sentenced him so harshly.

In a series of violent robberies, jailbreaks and shoot-outs with the police, John Dillinger earned himself the title of Public Enemy Number One. His bank raids with the "Terror Gang" – men he'd broken out of jail – were well-planned. Dillinger had studied the methods of a notorious Prussian ex-army officer turned bank-robber, Herman "The Baron" Lamm. The Baron believed that each bank he was going to rob should be treated like a military target. One of the gang, called the "jugman," was sent to spy on the chosen bank, making notes about everything he saw. The other gang members were each given a special task and had to do their homework. For instance, the getaway driver had to study maps and memorize his escape routes. Everything was timed to the second.

Dillinger robbed 15 banks this way, seizing over $300,000. Although his crime spree only lasted 14 months, his escapades were followed by the American public with the same enthusiasm modern audiences give to soap operas. It was the depression era in America and times were hard for working men. The Wall Street Crash of October, 1929 had almost bankrupted the nation, and many people were destitute. Dillinger played on the public's dissatisfaction with the banks and the authorities to help them through the crisis. During one raid, he approached a farmer who was holding a roll of dollar bills.

"Is that your money or the bank's money?" Dillinger asked.

"Mine," replied the man.

"You can keep it then. We only take the bank's."

Dillinger tipped his hat to the ladies and exchanged jokes with the men during his robberies. His charm was legendary and he loved to show off his athleticism. He once asked his jugman to report on the height of a bank clerk's security barrier. When the jugman wanted to know the reason for this request, Dillinger only laughed. At the next raid, he vaulted over the seven-foot barrier like a high jumper. It became his trademark feat at every bank robbery and he was nicknamed "the Jack Rabbit" in newspaper reports.

Although Dillinger became a hero figure to some poor Americans, he was still a mercenary gangster and would kill to save his skin. In January 1934, a bank raid in East Chicago, Indiana, went badly wrong. A brave clerk sounded the alarm and, by the time Dillinger got outside, police officer William O'Malley had arrived on the scene. He shot the gangster twice in the chest. But Dillinger was wearing a bulletproof vest. The policeman had no such protection: Dillinger machine-gunned him down.

After this murder, the police stepped up their efforts to catch the Jack Rabbit. But Dillinger was always one step ahead of them – and he had an escape plan. He contacted friends in Chicago, Illinois, and offered $5,000 to any criminal doctor who would perform plastic surgery to alter his features. In a nightmarish operation, with only a partial anaesthetic, he had the skin over his cheeks lifted, two moles removed and a dimple on his chin filled with tissue taken from his ears.

Soon, he would be able to walk the streets without the constant risk of being identified and challenged by the police. He even had a new girlfriend, Polly Hamilton. And he also enjoyed the company of her landlady, Anna Sage.

Dillinger didn't know it, but Sage was in desperate trouble. In 1933, she had been arrested for running a bar without a permit and the government wanted to send her back to Romania, where she was born. But Sage had a teenage son in America and would do anything to stay in the country. Polly Hamilton had been a waitress in Sage's bar and, when she turned up one night with the most-wanted man in America on her arm, Sage saw a chance to save herself.

She telephoned the head of Chicago's FBI department, Melvin Purvis. "I can get you Dillinger," she promised him. "But I want something in return."

Purvis was in trouble himself. The director of the FBI, J. Edgar Hoover, was threatening to replace him if he didn't catch Public Enemy Number One. He hastily arranged a secret meeting with the new informant.

Sage told Purvis that Dillinger loved to watch gangster movies with Polly and herself, and he visited her apartment every few days. If Purvis would cancel the deportation order, she would phone him the next time Dillinger stopped by. Purvis needed her help. Two months earlier he'd lost an agent in a botched raid at a remote lodge, after a gun battle with the Terror Gang. His men had accidentally shot three bystanders, killing one of them, and the gangsters had escaped. Purvis offered his resignation after this disaster but Hoover had refused it, demanding instead some quick results. Purvis told Sage he would try to help with the deportation case, but warned her that he couldn't make any promises.

"It's a deal," said Sage. "We always go to either the 'Marbro' or the 'Biograph.' Wait for my call and I'll tell you which it is."

Purvis was a small, light-bodied man who was seen as hardworking and courageous by his colleagues. He knew this was the best chance he had to catch an unsuspecting Dillinger. The day after meeting Sage, he summoned every agent he could muster to his downtown headquarters. At 5:00pm, his private phone rang. It was Sage, phoning from the delicatessen below her apartment. "But I still don't know which place we're going to," she added, before hanging up the phone.

Purvis had to split his army of FBI men into two squads and send them to both movie houses. He decided that Dillinger and the women were more likely to visit the Biograph as it was closer to Sage's apartment, but he couldn't take any chances. Half his men went to the Marbro and Purvis set off in a car for the Biograph.

The July heat was stifling as Purvis waited with his team of agents opposite the Biograph entrance. The hours passed and still there was no sign of their quarry. The FBI man knew that Dillinger had changed his appearance. He needed Sage to identify him by holding the gangster's arm as they approached the ticket booth. Purvis had asked her to wear a red dress so his men would notice her in the crowd of people milling around in the street. They scoured the pedestrians for the lady in a red dress for almost three hours. Then, suddenly, at around 8:15pm, one of the detectives spotted her. She was with another woman and a man, his arms linked between theirs – it must be Dillinger. The man paid for some tickets and the trio darted inside.

Purvis quickly contacted his men at the Marbro and ordered them to join him, then he hurried across the street and bought a ticket. But he was too late. Once inside the darkened auditorium it was impossible to see where the group was sitting. Rather than call attention to himself by staring at the faces of the audience, Purvis slipped outside and took up a position by the entrance. Like his men, Purvis was wearing a long jacket to conceal his gun holster, and the heat was almost unbearable. He would have to wait for two hours or more, until the end of the film, ready to light a cigar as soon as Dillinger passed. This was the signal for the other agents to make their move. There were now almost 20 FBI agents circling the building.

It was a nerve-wracking vigil for the anxious Purvis. He was so jumpy he chewed his unlit cigar until it was pulp, and this gave him a raging thirst. But he couldn't leave his post to gulp a glass of water. Dillinger might decide to leave the movie early and Purvis risked another failure if he dropped his guard, even for a second. His future with the FBI, and the lives of his men, were on the line.

Finally, the house manager became so suspicious of the loitering detective that he telephoned the police. As soon as they arrived in a marked police car, FBI agents ran over and warned them away. It was a close call. Just as the police were backing away, the Biograph audience began to pour out onto the street.

Purvis craned his neck trying to spot the woman in red. There were hundreds of people pushing past him, and he had to stand on tiptoe to catch a glimpse of his target. Then he heard a man's voice behind him.

"Ladies, that was a swell movie."

He swung around. It was Dillinger, only inches away, staring straight into his eyes. The gangster shuffled past him in the crowd and Purvis lit a match and held it to his cigar. The agents rushed in.

"Stick 'em up, Johnnie, we have you surrounded," called Purvis, in a voice he later admitted was high-pitched and squeaky because of his nerves.

Dillinger realized the women he'd been with had slipped away into the throng. He threw himself to the side and sprinted in the direction of a back alley. But the FBI wasn't going to miss the Jack Rabbit this time. The gangster was shot twice and died instantly.

A crowd gathered around his corpse. When they heard it was Dillinger lying before them, some of them were so awed by the sight of this near-legendary gangster that they dipped their fingertips in the spreading pool of his still-warm blood.

Although the capture and shooting of John Dillinger was a triumph for the FBI, few of the people involved went on to have happy or successful lives. Two women bystanders were shot and slightly wounded during the chase into the alleyway. Anna Sage received $5,000 in reward money but she was eventually deported, despite the best efforts of Purvis. She died in Romania of liver failure in 1947. Purvis retired from the FBI a year after the Biograph shooting. Following a failed business career, he was killed in 1960 by a bullet from the very gun that his fellow agents had presented to him on his resignation from the FBI. It is still unclear whether his death was a suicide or an accident. Polly Hamilton went back to waitressing in bars, and one of the agents who shot Dillinger, Herman Hollis, was himself cut down during a gun battle on November 27, 1934, tackling the last member of the Terror Gang. At least all these people could console themselves with the fact that they had helped to trap the most dangerous man in America. Or could they?

In 1979, an old Canadian bank robber, "Blackie" Audett, claimed that a few days after the Biograph shooting, he drove a live-and-kicking Dillinger to Oregon and left the gangster on an isolated Indian reservation, with $70,000 to start a new life. Audett even produced a 1948 snapshot of a man he said was John Dillinger. Historians have mocked Audett's claims, but there remain a number of nagging questions about the identity of the man shot down outside the Biograph...

As part of his new disguise, Dillinger had begun wearing glasses, although he had perfect vision. But the glasses found outside the Biograph were fitted with prescription lenses. Dillinger might have worn reading glasses or plain, glass lenses, but it would be odd if he had gone to the trouble and discomfort of wearing prescription lenses. During the police autopsy, it was revealed that the dead man had a surgical scar on his abdomen. But Dillinger had never had an operation that would leave such a scar. The man's eyes were described as being brown: Dillinger's eyes were a smoky blue. Another curious discovery was that the dead man had suffered problems with his heart since childhood. But Dillinger was an athlete and had never complained of any heart pain. He had also taken a full, navy medical examination when he joined the service and there was no record then of any heart condition.

Historians are still arguing with one another over this mystery. Most believe that it was Dillinger who died at the Biograph. His sister identified the body the morning after the shooting. But to this day criminals from the Chicago underworld whisper that Dillinger, the man who always had a plan, had arranged for someone to impersonate him that evening.

Perhaps, at this moment, a very old man is tending his garden in a remote corner of Oregon, still chuckling about his lucky escape.

The Dutchman meets Murder Inc.

Arthur Flegenheimer was always curious about religion. At different stages of his life he was an Orthodox Jew, a Protestant and a Catholic. Flegenheimer wanted to keep all his options open. As one of New York's biggest gang bosses, with a score of enemies, perhaps he thought he needed all the help he could get.

Arthur was born in 1902, in a rough area called the Bronx in the northeast of the city. He enjoyed school and might have made it to college, but when he was 14 his father abandoned the family. To help make ends meet, Arthur gave up his lessons and found a job. He soon discovered that delivering papers and working as an office boy was too much like hard work. Arthur preferred lounging around pool halls and dreaming of becoming a gangster millionaire. Short of cash, he joined a gang and started robbing houses.

Arthur's first and only prison term was the result of one of these burglaries. At 17, he was sent to the brutal Blackwell's Island Penitentiary, stranded in the middle of New York's East River. He was a disruptive and violent prisoner, and his sentence was extended when he escaped from his cell – only to be recaptured within a few hours. After 15 months behind bars he returned to the Bronx, toughened by his experiences. His gangster friends renamed him "Dutch Schultz," or the "Dutchman." This was a reference to a notorious street-fighter from the 1800s, one of the violent Frog Hollow Gang. Schultz was short and slight in stature, but he had a ferocious temper and would never back down in a fight. It was this aggressive, stubborn streak that would eventually get him killed.

Between crimes, Schultz took the occasional honest job. He was working for a small trucking business with a friend named Joey Noe, when a group of bootleggers hired them to distribute kegs of beer. Dutch soon realized what huge profits the gangsters were making. It cost only $3 to brew a keg of beer. This was sold to distributors, or salesmen, for $9 and by the time it got to the speakeasy it fetched $19. The only problem with bootlegging was that you had to be prepared to fight for a share of the market. But this didn't worry Schultz for a moment.

Joey Noe and the Dutchman opened a chain of speakeasies at the end of the 1920s. Noe understood the buying and trucking side of the business, and Schultz took care of the muscle. His fearsome reputation encouraged most gangsters not to mess with him. To increase their profits, the two friends bought their beer from a brewer outside New York, and found three trucks to carry it into the city. Schultz sometimes rode along in one of the trucks, hugging a machine gun to discourage hijackers. With the money pouring in, the two friends decided it was time to expand their empire.

Schultz had a simple method for promoting their beer. He'd visit a rival speakeasy with his gang and order a round of drinks. As soon as he took a sip he'd spit it on the floor.

"This stuff's undrinkable," he'd tell the barman. "From now on, you're going to buy your beer from Joey and me."

If the barman didn't like the idea, Schultz and his gang would set fire to the place. Within a few months, Schultz and Noe were controlling all the speakeasies in the Bronx. Of course, there were some bootleggers who resented these interlopers. One of them was a tough gangster named Joe Rock. He vowed he'd never surrender control of his speakeasies, especially to a pipsqueak like Dutch. So Schultz kidnapped Joe and dangled him from a hook by his thumbs. He was beaten and tortured, and his family had to pay a ransom of $35,000 to release him. It was dangerous to say "no" to the Dutchman.

For a while, all went well for the two bootlegging buddies. But when they launched their business in Manhattan, Noe was gunned down outside his hotel. Even though he was wearing a bulletproof vest, he was badly injured and died after wasting away in the hospital for over a month. Bootlegger Jack "Legs" Diamond was the chief suspect for the shooting. He was furious about Dutch and Noe's incursion into his territory. Diamond was nicknamed "the Clay Pigeon" because of the number of times he'd been shot: he survived half a dozen assassination attempts, and was blasted 14 times in all, before he was finally killed in December, 1931.

Schultz was crushed by the death of his friend. But in true gangster style he got on with business. After all, with Noe gone, the Dutchman inherited his partner's share of the empire. He was now the biggest bootlegger in town, "the Beer Baron of New York," and still only at the beginning of his career.

By 1929, Schultz was so important in the New York gangs that he was invited to meetings with the boss of bosses, Lucky Luciano. It was the beginning of "the Syndicate," a new union of gang leaders from all racial backgrounds, and Schultz was asked to vote at their gatherings. One of their decisions was to establish a new business: Murder Incorporated. It was a startling idea, and one that would have terrible consequences for the Dutchman.

Murder Inc. was set up by the gang leaders of the Syndicate in response to a pressing problem. They were finding it difficult to hire efficient and reliable assassins.

Gangs had always used violence and murder as important business tools. In some situations, it became necessary to "remove" an individual permanently. He or she might be an inconvenient witness to a murder, or a gangster who had been arrested and was threatening to talk to the police. Sometimes, people approached gang bosses and asked them if they could arrange a murder for a fee. But it wasn't always easy to find skilled assassins from within the ranks of a gang. Strange as it might seem, most gangsters had too many scruples to be clinical killing machines. Also, there were risks if the killers were locals. The police or potential witnesses might recognize them. Friends of the victim would be able to guess who was responsible. For this reason, many gangs used outside killers to do their dirty work. Murder Inc. was merely an extension of this tactic.

The business of assassination was not an original

idea. Gangs of hired killers have been around for centuries. The word "assassin" itself was first coined during the Crusades in the Middle Ages, probably from the name of a drug which drove fighters into a murdering frenzy. The word became linked to stories of shadowy religious groups who were devoted to killing. The members of one sect were so loyal to their leader, the "Old Man of the Mountain", that they would throw themselves from the lofty ramparts of his castle on his orders. Another assassin cult, the Thugs, strangled victims on the lonely roadways of India during the 1800s. They were motivated by their religious beliefs, but some of them also carried out assassinations for money. So the New York gangs were carrying on a long tradition when they founded Murder Inc.

Schultz had no objections to the new business. Its rules were simple. A number of New York assassins would be kept on a fixed wage and would not have to do any work for their masters other than murder. Because they were unknown to their victims, it made it very difficult for the police to link them to their crimes. They were not allowed to kill public officials (as this could bring unwelcome publicity) or high-ranking gangsters without the permission of the Syndicate board, who would take a vote on the matter. If the Syndicate thought an assassination was too risky, they could veto it.

Most important of all, the men selected had to be cold-hearted killing machines. One of the most monstrous Murder Inc. personnel was Abe "Kid Twist" Reles. This gangster was only five feet two inches tall, but he was immensely powerful. He was a strangler: his fingers could crush a raw potato into pulp. What's more, Reles enjoyed his job. He was tough, and had been shot several times and survived. This man, and others just as dangerous, were the core members of Murder Incorporated.

But Dutch Schultz had other things to think about than this new business. One of his gang lieutenants, Vincent "Mad Dog" Coll, was demanding a larger share of the Dutchman's profits. Schultz refused, and Coll split from the gang and waged war against his former employer. Only after a series of bloody gun battles did Dutch triumph over Coll. With the easy-money from the Prohibition era coming to an end, he immediately turned his attention to new money-making schemes.

Dutch invaded the gambling dens of Harlem, New York, where thousands of people played a game called "the numbers," a bit like a modern lottery. The game was organized by dozens of small operators, who were powerless to stop the Dutchman from moving in and taking control. Any objections were met with the usual violence.

His next target was the restaurant trade. One of Schultz's men, Jules Martin, stood as a union leader for the North Manhattan Waiters Association. Once he was voted in — a corrupt contest where Martin won more votes than there were members of the union – Schultz took over other districts and began demanding annual fees from every restaurant owner. There were one-off charges to be paid as well, to avoid strikes or "accidents." If an owner refused to cooperate, he might be stink-bombed – which meant gangsters dropping a container full of disgustingly smelly chemicals down the restaurant chimney. The chemicals wrecked all the furniture and room fittings, and the smell soaked into the carpets and even the floor. It could take months of cleaning and expensive refitting before the restaurant reopened. It was the old Schultz tactic: meet resistance with brute force, and never back down.

Every dollar mattered to the Dutchman. Years later, when he suspected that Martin was dipping into the gang's bank accounts, Schultz slapped him in the face. When Martin at once confessed to taking a much smaller amount than Schultz thought was missing, Schultz shot him dead. He had a reputation for being miserly. At one of his court appearances he told the judge he never spent more than $35 on a suit. A newspaper reporter described him as looking like "an ill-dressed vagrant." Schultz was a millionaire several times over, but he still counted his pennies.

Yet the Schultz fortune was under threat. The gangster had failed to submit his annual tax forms and officials were demanding he pay $92,000. There was the threat of a long jail sentence if he was found guilty of tax evasion. So Schultz went into hiding for almost two years, only turning himself in to the police in November 1934, when he had finished making preparations for his case.

At his tax trial, witnesses displayed a surprising reluctance to give evidence against the gangster. Some of them claimed to have forgotten everything they'd told the police; others went missing altogether. It seemed that Schultz had "encouraged" them to forget. So the trial collapsed.

But the authorities wouldn't give up. They ordered a retrial in the small town of Malone, near the Canadian border. Their hope was that, outside New York, the gangster wouldn't be able to use his influence to silence witnesses.

Schultz fought back. He arrived in Malone a week before the case was due to begin and tried to win the sympathy of the local community. He hired a hall and offered free refreshments, including alcohol, while he explained to the townspeople that he was an innocent man. To the amazement of the government legal team, after a two-week-long trial the jury's verdict was "Not Guilty."

It wasn't just the tax men who were shocked by this outcome. Lucky Luciano had never expected Schultz to escape jail, and had already reassigned the Dutchman's criminal empire to various members of the Syndicate. Luciano did the decent thing, and handed it back to Schultz. But the Dutchman wasn't out of trouble yet. The District Attorney, Thomas

Dewey, was on a mission to clean up New York, and Schultz was his first target.

By 1935, Dutch Schultz was tired of the hounding he was getting from the authorities. He'd fought two trials and won, but now the District Attorney wanted to start a new case against him. Enough was enough. It was time for the tried and tested tactics he'd employed since he was a teenage bootlegger.

The Dutchman summoned one of the Murder Inc. assassins, Albert "the Mad Hatter" Anastasia.

"I want you to take out Dewey," he told him. "Find out how we can get at him."

But Dewey was an important public official, and Schultz knew he'd have to get permission for the murder from the other Syndicate members. So Anastasia presented his research to the assembled gang leaders. Every morning, Dewey went to the same drug shop with his bodyguards. The District Attorney called his office while the bodyguards waited outside. A Murder Inc. specialist could wait in the shop, shoot Dewey while he made his call and then escape through the back door.

Schultz was a senior member of the Syndicate and his request had to be taken seriously. Nonetheless, the other gang leaders decided it was far too dangerous to kill Dewey. It would only lead to more pressure from the authorities. They turned Schultz down. But the Bronx gangster was tired of being ordered around.

"I'll organize it myself if I have to!" he roared.

"Dewey will be dead within 48 hours." And he stormed out of the meeting.

After a moment's silence, Luciano raised his hand. "Gentlemen, I think we have no alternative. We must kill the Dutchman."

The Murder Inc. team pulled up outside the Palace Chop House in Newark on October 23, 1935. They were Charles "the Bug" Workman, "Mendy" Weiss and a driver, known only as "Piggy." The assassins had been told that Schultz was inside with three of his men. There was no time for any subtlety. Workman and Weiss stepped into the restaurant and started shooting.

The Dutchman's gang – bodyguards Lulu Rosenkrantz and Abe Landau, and his accountant, "Abbadabba" Berman – were surprised at one of the tables, but managed to grab their guns and return fire. While Weiss shot it out with them, Workman ran through to the rear bathrooms and found Dutch drying his hands. The assassin shot him down before the gang boss could say a word.

Back in the restaurant, the bullets were flying. Rosenkrantz was hit seven times, Berman six and Landau three. Somehow, they still managed to stagger to their feet and drive the assassins out into the street. In the meantime, Dutch stumbled into the room and shouted for a doctor. Rosenkrantz, bleeding terribly, lurched over to the bar and slammed a coin down.

"Give me change for the phone," he croaked at the

shaking bartender. The terrified man did as he was told, and the bodyguard called the ambulance service before passing out on the floor.

Rosenkrantz must have been a tough customer. As he lay dying on his hospital bed, a detective interrogated him.

"Who shot you?" he demanded.

"I don't know," answered Rosenkrantz. "Now go out and get me an ice-cream soda." He was the last of the men to die.

The Dutchman had been shot once, in his left side. The high velocity bullet had wrecked his intestines and internal organs so badly, it was incredible he even made it to the hospital. Surgeons tried to save him, but it was hopeless. For 24 hours he drifted in and out of consciousness, finally summoning a Catholic priest to give him the last rites.

A few hours before his death, he began to mutter a strange poetry of gangster expressions and broken words. Some of his speech was gibberish, but there were whole sentences and parts of a conversation hidden in his continuous drawl. The police recorded every word in case it might help them track down his killers. This stream of words has been studied by authors and students as a unique example of the American language. The author, William Burroughs, even wrote an experimental book based on it: *The Last Words of Dutch Schultz*. One example of Schultz's utterances was: "Mother is the best bet and don't let Satan draw you too fast."

The Dutchman passed away at 8:35pm, the day after the shooting. He had finally met his match against the guns of Murder Incorporated. He was 33 years old.

We know about Schultz's assassination from the testimony of a surprise gangster witness: Kid Twist Reles. Reles had been arrested in 1940 on a murder charge and, when he realized he didn't stand a chance of escaping life in prison, or even execution, he made a deal with the government. Reles had a good memory. He described over 80 Murder Inc. killings, giving the police every detail in each case.

Following Reles' testimony, Charles "the Bug" Workman was sentenced to life in prison for his part in the Schultz murder. Mendy Weiss was found guilty of another murder and electrocuted at Ossining Prison (better known as "Sing Sing") in 1944.

Kid Twist revealed everything about Murder Inc. From his statements, the police estimated the company had carried out at least 200 murders. Reles was linked to many of them, but hoped that by giving evidence he would be spared execution.

It was not to be. As the evidence began to implicate more powerful gangsters – Bugsy Siegel among them – Kid Twist became a serious threat to the Syndicate. Then, in November 1941, he was killed. He dropped from his sixth-floor hotel room in

Coney Island. There was a length of knotted sheets attached to the window sill. His room was locked from the inside and guarded by six police officers, but there was no evidence to suggest he took his own life. An inquiry decided it was "death by misadventure." Nobody was ever prosecuted for the murder. Perhaps Kid Twist had been trying to escape or play a practical joke on his guards. Or perhaps another assassin had done his job only too well.

Nothing can be worth this...

The man in the blindfold fell out of the car and struggled to his feet. He could feel a light drizzle on his face. The night air was cold and there was no sound except for the patter of the rain on the highway. He guessed they were out in the middle of the prairie.

"Are you going to kill me?" the man mumbled, trying to keep his nerve. For nine days he'd been chained to a bed, his eyes covered, unable to sleep he was so terrified of what the kidnappers might do.

"I will if you talk to the police," a voice growled from the car. "Now turn around and start walking. There's a gas station down the road. When you get there, you can take the blindfold off and call for a ride home."

The man turned away from the car and staggered into the rain. From behind the steering wheel, the gangster watched him vanish into the gloom of the Oklahoma night. The gangster was smiling. The ransom was paid, all $200,000 of it, and his victim had never taken his blindfold off, so what could he tell the FBI about his kidnappers or their hideout? The gang was in the clear.

The gangster started the engine and pulled onto the highway. But, before accelerating away, he hesitated. Would it have been safer to shoot Urschel, as the gang had first discussed? There was still time to do it. He glanced over at the menacing shape of his Thompson sub-machine gun, nestled on the rear seat. Then the old bank-robber and bootlegger shook his head. He didn't want to kill a man in cold blood, and besides, he was sure that Urschel couldn't do him any harm. The gangster laughed and gunned the engine.

The other man heard the laugh and the roar of the car engine, fading into the distance. He had good ears. As the gang that had kidnapped him was about to learn, Charles F. Urschel had very good ears indeed.

His ordeal had begun on July 22, 1933. Every Saturday night, Urschel and his wife, Berenice, played cards with their friends, the Jarretts. Charles and Berenice were one of the richest couples in Oklahoma City. They were part of the "black gold aristocracy" – oil millionaires. Their marriage had joined two oil empires; Charles was a self-made man in the industry, and Berenice was the widow of a maverick oil-prospector, "the king of the wildcatters," Tom Slick. The Urschels had one of the finest mansions in the area and, because the night was warm, they had been sitting out on the porch to finish their game of bridge. It was Berenice who first noticed the two intruders, stepping out of the shadows. One of them lifted a machine gun level to the card table. Berenice screamed.

"Nobody make another sound or I'll blow your heads off," hissed the gunman. "Which one of you men is Urschel?"

There was silence. Walter Jarrett had no intention of betraying his friend.

"We'll take both of you then," the man snarled, and he dragged Urschel and Jarrett across the lawn and towards a parked car. It was all over in seconds, and the two women were left wondering if they'd ever see their husbands alive again.

After driving several miles on rough dirt roads, the car stopped and the kidnappers jumped out.

"Let's see your wallets," demanded one of them.

The ID photos in the wallets gave the game away. Walter Jarrett was abandoned at the side of the road, his purse pilfered of the $51 he'd been carrying. The car took off and Urschel watched as one of the kidnappers brought out a blindfold and adhesive tape.

"You've seen enough for tonight. Close your eyes," the man ordered.

Urschel was scared and did as he was told. But then he felt a rush of anger. How dare these men break into the grounds of his own house and point a gun in his wife's face? They'd go to jail for this, if he had anything to do with it. He let the man blindfold him, but he was determined that he'd have some facts about his attackers to tell the police – if he survived. Urschel had a good memory. With his eyes covered he suddenly became conscious of all the sounds inside and outside the car, the stops they had to make, and even the smell of the country air. If he forced himself to remember everything about their journey, he might be able to give the police a "picture" of his abduction, even without use of his sight.

Urschel began by estimating the time he'd been in the car. He knew when he'd been kidnapped, and by carefully measuring his breathing (guessing that each deep breath took about ten seconds) he calculated how many minutes passed between each one of his "memory signposts." After an hour of driving, he could tell from the smell – he knew it well – that they were passing through an oil field. Two hours later, the car stopped and one of the men got out to open a gate. Two hours after this, they changed cars and Urschel was hidden under the rear seat of the new car. After another hour's driving, they swerved into a gas station and Urschel eavesdropped on the kidnappers' conversation with a woman attendant.

"Oh," he heard her say, "the crops around here are all burned up from too much sun."

Finally, after an eternity cramped in the back of the car, they parked and killed the engine. Urschel was led into a building and told to lie down on an iron bed. He made a careful mental note of everything he'd heard that night, before giving in to his exhaustion and tumbling into sleep.

Over the next nine days, Urschel concentrated on every detail of his sightless, sensory experience. Like a human tape recorder, he noted every detail, no matter how trivial it seemed.

He knew there was quite a big gang involved, as he detected several voices. They were mostly men but one woman was staying there as well, although she was never in the same room with him. He knew also that he was a prisoner on a working farm, as he could hear cows, pigs and chickens in the surrounding fields. The food he ate was dull and the drinking water had a powerful, mineral taste. Each time a man went to fetch some with a bucket, Urschel heard the creaking of an old well-handle.

Urschel soon noticed that a plane flew over the

farm twice a day, at about the same times. Craftily, when he next heard the plane, he asked one of his guards what time it was, but only after waiting ten minutes to avoid any suspicion. He did the same thing with the later flight, and was able to deduce that the planes crossed the sky overhead at approximately 9:45am and 5:45pm. In addition to this, Urschel remembered every storm or shower and tried to calculate the precise times they happened. On July 30, for example, he heard a violent rainstorm. He waited for the morning plane to arrive but it never came.

Urschel fastidiously stored all this information in his memory. He bided his time and did nothing to provoke the anger of his captors. On the morning of July 31, he was bundled into a car and, after several hours of driving, was released into the pouring rain. The next day he was at home, being interviewed by the FBI.

The detectives already had some suspects for the kidnapping: George "Machine Gun" Kelly and his gang. Two Texas policemen had warned the FBI about an earlier abduction the gang had been planning, and when agents had shown Kelly's prison mug shots to Berenice, she identified him as one of the card-game intruders. The FBI studied the personality of the man they were up against.

He was born George Kelly Barnes in Chicago in 1900. His family moved to Memphis when he was two, and he had a comfortable childhood, although his relationship with his father was rocky, to say the least. When he was a young man and his first marriage was failing, Kelly tried to kill himself by drinking a chemical solution of mercury. He telephoned his father and told him what he'd done.

"When I'm dead, will you bury me?" he asked him.

"Gladly, son," answered his father.

The years leading up to his attempted suicide were cursed with laziness and bad luck. Kelly had been to college but dropped out before the end of the first year. He drifted into bootlegging and petty crime until he fell in love with Geneva Ramsey and made an effort to settle down. It almost worked. Geneva's father, George, gave Kelly a job in his railroad construction company and the two men worked hard to develop the business. But one day George was blown to pieces by a stick of dynamite and Kelly – and the business – never recovered. He started drinking, made the failed suicide attempt and Geneva divorced him.

Years of heavy drinking and trouble with the law followed. Kelly might have fought back to reclaim his family and a respectful life and triumphed but, before he could pull himself together, he had another stroke of bad luck. He met a bootlegger's moll, Kathryn Thorne, and fell in love and married again. Kelly didn't know it, but his new wife was poison.

Kathryn had been in and out of prison all her life.

She'd been married three times to gangsters and bootleggers, one of whom died in mysterious circumstances after Kathryn discovered he'd been seeing another woman. Wild and dangerous, she'd always wanted a rich gangster for a husband. It was Kathryn who created the legend around Kelly, that he was a crack-shot machine-gunner, trained by the U.S. army – a real stone-hearted killer. She even gave her friends spent machine-gun cartridges, saying they were Kelly's "calling card." Kathryn boasted her new husband was such a dead shot, he could shoot a walnut off a fence post at 45m (50 yards).

The truth was quite different. Kelly was a chubby, affable man who'd never been in the army, never killed anyone and was more of a court-jester than a sharpshooter. But Kathryn was determined to build up his gangster reputation. She gave him the name "Machine Gun," bragged about his criminal talents to anyone who'd listen, and persuaded him to start robbing banks. Finding the takings of Depression-hit country banks weren't enough to satisfy her greed, she began planning a kidnapping. The ransom would enable the Kellys to retire to Mexico and live in luxury. But kidnapping was a risky business: it meant taking on the might of the FBI.

In 1932, a crime was committed that shocked the entire American nation. The baby son of the world-famous aviator Charles Lindbergh (the first person to fly solo across the Atlantic, in 1927) was kidnapped from the family home in New Jersey. The kidnapping dominated the newspapers for almost two months, until the body of the victim was discovered only a few miles from the scene of the kidnapping. The sense of outrage after the Lindbergh abduction and murder encouraged the government to make kidnapping a federal (or national) crime. This allowed the FBI to investigate such cases, if it was considered possible that the criminal had crossed a state boundary. Before this, kidnapping investigations had been left to small and sometimes poorly-equipped local police forces. To drive their message home further, politicians decided the maximum jail sentence for kidnapping should be increased to "life."

The Kelly gang didn't consider the dangers of their new gangster business. They were only thinking about the money they could make. While Urschel had been a prisoner at their hideout, they'd sent a series of notes to Berenice and successfully collected the ransom (delivered by one of Urschel's most-trusted friends). Back at their hideout they were celebrating, before dividing up the loot and going their separate ways. But now the FBI agents were on their trail and their days of freedom were numbered.

The agents began their investigation with an examination of airline schedules for every flight within a 1,000km (600-mile) radius of Oklahoma City. After poring over the schedules, they came across two American Airlines flights that departed daily at 9:15am and 3:30pm. By cross-referencing the flights to see where they'd be after 15 minutes of flying, the FBI agents guessed that the gang's hideout must be close to the town of Paradise, Texas. To double-check their finding, they contacted the local weather service and discovered that, on the morning of July 30, the 9:15am flight had been diverted to avoid a severe storm. The meteorologist also told them that Paradise had suffered a dry corn season, and the crops were damaged.

Urschel's hard work was paying off.

Next, the agents studied their files on the Kelly gang, to see if any of their families or associates had links to Paradise, Texas. Kathryn Kelly's stepfather, Robert "Boss" Shannon, owned a farm nearby. The FBI wondered if this could be a coincidence.

On August 10, an agent posing as a salesman visited the farm to see if it matched Urschel's description. The layout of the buildings was identical and there were plenty of animals in the surrounding fields. The agent knocked on the door and, after chatting with the owner for a while, asked for a drink of water. He heard a loud grating noise from the well-handle and the water had a sour, mineral aftertaste.

As soon as they could muster their forces, the FBI raided the farm and arrested several gang members. Kathryn Kelly's mother, who lived there with Boss Shannon, was also taken into custody. Within minutes, one of the Shannon family had made a full confession. Urschel, armed with a shotgun, even identified some of his kidnappers from their voices. But the leaders of the gang, Kelly and Kathryn, had already flown.

By now, the kidnapping was the biggest news story in the country. On the run and under pressure, Kathryn started to crack. Showing her true character, she wrote a vicious and sneaky letter to Joseph Keenan, the government prosecutor of the case:

> *The entire Urschel family and friends... will be exterminated soon. I will gladly put George Kelly on the spot for you if you will save my mother...*

Kathryn wanted to pin the crime on Kelly. This would help her family and, more importantly, save her from spending the rest of her life in prison. Kelly, confused and panicky now the FBI was hunting him, started drinking gin. He wrote his own letters to his pursuers. From a highway motel hideout, he even sent one to Charles Urschel. It began:

> *Just a few lines to let you know I am getting my plans made to destroy your mansion and you and your family...*

In the rambling letter, he warned Urschel to drop the charges against him and promised revenge if he was imprisoned. At the bottom of the page he left his fingerprints in ink, adding: *so you can't say some crank wrote this.* He signed off: *see you in Hell.*

It was another piece of Kelly bad luck. He would live to regret writing these threatening words to his kidnapping victim.

The ransom had been paid in $20 bills and all their serial numbers had been recorded by the FBI. By following the trail of where these marked notes were spent, and intercepting the desperate telegrams between the Kellys and their associates, it didn't take the FBI long to locate the gangsters.

On September 26, a team of detectives kicked down the door of a tumbledown house in Memphis, Tennessee. Machine Gun Kelly was arrested in the bathroom, still wearing his nightclothes. He was bleary-eyed and hungover from his gin drinking.

"I've been waiting for you all night," he muttered, as the handcuffs clicked into place.

The trial of the Urschel kidnappers was the first to be recorded on movie cameras. In the film, Kelly looks tense and fidgety, whereas Kathryn clearly enjoyed her moment in the limelight. Her hair was carefully styled and she wore fashionable clothes. From the start, she exhibited her survival instincts, stressing that the kidnapping had been all "George's idea." She claimed she had begged Kelly to release Urschel as soon as she'd found out about the kidnapping. She presented herself as an innocent victim of a violent and domineering man. Poor

George sat in silence, watching his wife trying to blame him for everything.

But all her lies and acting ability in the witness stand didn't help Kathryn one bit. The rest of the gang had already told the jury about her active roll in the planning and execution of the kidnapping.

On October 12, the Kellys were sentenced to life in a federal jail.

George jumped to his feet. "I'll bust out before Christmas," he screamed, in a last act of bravado. "No prison can hold me," he bellowed as they were taking him away.

This outburst so alarmed the authorities, they decided to send Kelly to the maximum security prison, Alcatraz. With little chance of a jailbreak from the island, Kelly passed his days boasting to fellow inmates about his crimes. The other prisoners soon named him "Popgun" Kelly, in mockery of the hard-man moniker Kathryn had given him.

He died in Leavenworth prison, of a heart attack, on July 17, 1954.

Kathryn was more hardy. She was released on parole in 1958 and immediately requested a retrial, alleging that some of the FBI's evidence at the first trial had been unreliable. Because the FBI refused to surrender their case files, she was set free. She took a job in an Oklahoma hospital and became a recluse. After her mother died, she disappeared from sight and her fate is unknown.

During the long years he spent on Alcatraz, Machine Gun Kelly had ample time to reflect on his mistakes, his bad luck and his disappointing criminal career. In an attempt to win parole, he wrote to Charles Urschel over and over again, begging him to forgive his kidnapper and to put in a good word with the authorities. But Urschel's memory was still good. He had saved Kelly's note threatening him and his family. He wasn't in a forgiving mood.

Machine Gun Kelly always wanted a second chance in life, but he never got it. In a last letter to Urschel, Kelly wrote:

five words are written in fire on the walls of my cell: NOTHING CAN BE WORTH THIS! This is the final word of wisdom so far as crime is concerned.

The oil baron was unmoved. He visited Alcatraz to meet the convict, but he only made the journey to ask questions about his missing ransom money. Kelly didn't know where it was. Some $80,000 was never recovered. It had probably been buried deep in a Texas oil field by one of the gang. So the oil-money ransom that had ruined so many lives may have found its way back into the ground.

The Australian iron gang

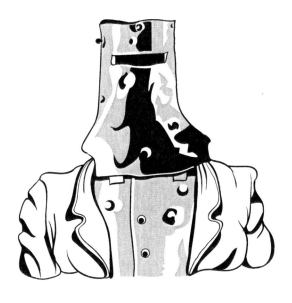

Out of the dawn mist it staggered, a strange shape tottering towards them. It was larger than any man, with a huge square head and a barrel chest. The policemen had been up all night, watching over the gang's hideout close to a remote railway station. Staring at the advancing figure, the sleepy men wondered if they were in the grip of a nightmare. The creature was made of iron!

They fired everything they had at it, but their bullets just bounced off the monstrous iron beast. In a panic, the policemen turned and got ready to run.

But one man, a gritty railway guard named Jesse Dowsett, stood his ground, aiming carefully at the legs of the monster. He saw his bullets cut into flesh and bone, and heard the awful screams coming from behind the iron mask. At last, when his revolver was almost empty, the metal man crumpled to the ground before him. Jesse ran over and tore the helmet away. Ned Kelly, the Australian gang leader, stared up at him with exhausted, bloodshot eyes.

Trapped inside the Glenrowan Inn only a short distance away, the three members of Kelly's gang were dead or dying. Like him, they were wearing iron suits which protected them in part but, where their flesh was exposed, they were vulnerable to police bullets. Handsome Joe Byrne was already dead, shot in the legs and the groin. Ned's teenage brother, Dan, and his best friend, Steve Hart, were wounded but still defiant, taunting the police and returning their fire. But they were encircled by 50 riflemen and their time was running short.

During the night, Ned had slipped out of the inn and found his faithful horse waiting for him. He could have escaped, but instead he'd returned to lead his gang on a last, desperate charge against their enemies. But the iron suit he wore weighed 40kg (90lbs). Although he was as strong as an ox, the loss of blood from his wounds, and the crushing burden of iron, had proved too much for him to bear.

Jesse Dowsett carried Ned into the railway station

hut and laid him on a table. A doctor cut away the leather thongs that secured the gangster's metal suit, and treated the wounds to his arms, legs, hands and feet. He'd lost so much blood the doctor thought Ned would be dead within the hour. As soon as the priest, Dean Gibley, arrived, he was asked to read the outlaw the last rites. Ned was polite and respectful to the priest, while in the background, rifle-cracks and revolver blasts echoed off the trees. It was the end of Australia's most famous and deadly gang. But not the end of Ned Kelly.

Kelly was born in the wild back country of the Australian state of Victoria, in December, 1854. Australia was a hard place in those days, and only the tough or the wealthy could flourish there. Kelly's parents came from the ranks of poor immigrants and convicts that the new land had absorbed, helping to build it into a great nation. "Red" Kelly, Ned's father, had been transported from Ireland for stealing two pigs. He'd served a seven-year prison sentence in Tasmania before settling near the town of Melbourne and meeting his wife, Ellen Quinn. Ellen had sailed from Ireland when she was only nine years old and, during the voyage, 16 other children and two adults had died of whooping cough. Ellen had been in Victoria for eight years before she married, and she understood only too well the harsh demands of her adopted country.

The Kelly family earned a living by hiring

themselves out to help clear new territory, and by trading in livestock. Despite all their efforts, most of the time they were extremely poor. The good pasture land had already been handed out to "squatters" by an earlier government. These squatters were immigrants like the Kellys, but they had been in the country longer, or had arrived with a fortune to invest in buying land. They jealously protected their estates and used the poor settlers almost as slave workers.

In an attempt to cultivate the vast areas that had been given to the squatters, the government permitted immigrants to "select" a few acres to farm. The squatters watched in fury as these "selectors" moved onto their land. Resentment between the two groups sometimes boiled over into violence, with an inefficient and occasionally corrupt police force caught in-between. One common source of disagreement was lost stock. Animals ranged over hundreds of miles, and the poor settlers claimed that any unbranded animal found wandering in the "bush" (the Australian forest and wilderness) belonged to the finder. Horses were particularly valuable. In a country with few roads and long distances between settlements, they were both a vital means of transport and a sign of status. The young Ned quite possibly learned how to ride before he could walk.

His health broken by years of hard work, Red Kelly died suddenly when Ned was 12, and the family moved to a remote area called Eleven Mile Creek. Ned grew up immersed in the tense atmosphere that existed between squatters and selectors. He became a master horseman and a dead shot by the time he was in his teens, learning to trust only his friends and to be suspicious of the police. Ned was hot-tempered, proud and physically powerful. But he had a tender side, and would risk his life to help others. He once jumped into a swollen river to rescue a boy from drowning. The boy's parents presented Ned with a fine, green silk sash for his bravery – Ned wore it under his iron suit when he made his last stand, trying to rescue his gang. The Kellys may have been poor and wary of authority, but they had a strict code of conduct. They looked after their own.

To keep her family in food and clothes, Ellen sold dinners and measures of brandy to miners, local farmers and people passing through the area. The Kelly house soon became a meeting place for poor working men and others who lived on the fringes of the law. After Ned got into a fight with a drunken Chinese miner, the local police chief, Superintendent Nicholson, warned his officers: "That house is an insult to our authority. We must drive the Kellys out and put them in prison."

Following another brawl, Ned was sentenced to six months in jail. The police crackdown on the Kellys had begun. Soon after his release, Ned was in more serious trouble. A man asked him to track down a lost horse, and Ned found it and proudly rode it into town. But the police had a description of the animal, as it had been stolen only a few days earlier. They seized Ned, without listening to his pleas, and beat him over the head with their pistol butts. He was found guilty of theft and sentenced to three years on a chain-gang. He was 16 years old.

The same ships that had carried the first convicts to Australia were still used as prison hulks, and Ned spent much of his sentence cooped-up inside the rotting decks of *HMS Battery*. During the day he built roads and quarried stone, burned by the fierce sun. In the evenings he lay inside his floating prison, at the mercy of swarms of mosquitoes. His life was under constant threat from disease, exhaustion and the violent attacks of guards and criminals. The young man grew angry and bitter at the way he'd been treated. But there was worse to come.

The authorities believed that if they could smash Ellen and her family, it would teach all the other selectors to be humble and law-abiding. Dan, one of Ned's brothers, was wanted for questioning about stealing a horse. On a quiet February night, not long after Ned had been released, a policeman named Fitzpatrick set out for the Kelly household. Perhaps the officer felt a chill in the air, because he stopped for a drink of brandy on his way. By the time he reached the house, he was tipsy. He bungled the arrest and cut his wrist in a struggle with Dan, who ran out into the night. On the way back to the police station, Officer Fitzpatrick stopped for another glass of brandy. When he made his report, he claimed that Ned Kelly had burst into the room, fired a shot at him and escaped. The whole family was accused of attempted murder. Dan hid in the bush with Ned, while Ellen was tried and sentenced to three years in prison.

This was the turning point for the young man who would soon become Australia's most renowned outlaw. Furious that his mother had been jailed on a trumped-up charge, Ned formed a gang. His plan was to rustle horses and raise enough money selling them to fight for Ellen's release. To this end, he recruited his lifelong friend, Joe Byrne, and former jockey, Steve Hart. Together, they rode deep into the bush, looking for somewhere safe to hide.

Ellen Kelly's prosecution was undeniably a brutal miscarriage of justice. Officer Fitzpatrick's evidence was untrustworthy – he was eventually thrown off the police force over a separate case of misconduct. But her punishment was not unexpected. This was a time of change in the new country, and the authorities were nervous about poor settlers wanting a better way of life. The squatters demanded long jail terms for trivial crimes, and the judges obliged. So while many of Ned's fellow countrymen saw his decision to form a gang as a brave stand for justice, the police were determined to destroy him. Kelly might not have known it but, as soon as he went on the run, he became an important symbol of revolt to both sides.

Large rewards were put out on the gang members, and in October, 1878, four policemen rode out from the town of Mansfield, close to where the gang was thought to be hiding. They were well armed with rifles, shotguns and ammunition, and they brought a pack horse with them. This pack horse was equipped with thick straps – ready to lash down the dead bodies of the Kelly gang.

It was a dangerous mission, because the police posse had underestimated their prey. Ned discovered their camp at Stringybark Creek, fetched his gang and surprised two of the sleepy policemen. In a short gunfight, Ned shot Officer Lonigan dead and captured Officer McIntyre. Suddenly, the rest of the posse rode into camp. Ned yelled "Bail up" – the Australian call to surrender. The police went for their guns and the Kelly gang, superior shots and bush fighters, finished them off. In the confusion, McIntyre escaped on a horse. When he reached Mansfield, he described how the Kelly gang had murdered the police in a cowardly ambush.

The Stringybark Creek Battle marked the beginning of the Kelly legend. To the police, he was a cold-blooded killer. To his supporters, he was a hounded man trying to defend himself. The authorities reacted to news of the shootings with customary force. They gave the police emergency powers to arrest anyone they suspected might be sympathetic to the gang. This was a tactical error. The public had had great sympathy for the police after the gunfight, but suddenly hundreds of people were locked up without trial and interrogated like criminals. This only added to the settlers' feeling that the police were being heavy-handed and Ned Kelly had simply been standing up for his rights.

Although he was safe in his bush hideout, Ned needed money. The gang's horse rustling wasn't earning as much cash as he'd hoped. He wanted to pay bail for friends and family who'd been arrested, and he was still trying to build a war chest of money he could use to help his jailed mother. At the same time, he still believed there were good and just men in the Australian government. He dictated a letter to Joe Byrne – Ned's writing skills were less advanced than his horsemanship – and sent it to a magistrate, asking for his help. This was only the first in a series of letters that the gang sent to the authorities, outlining their grievances and asking for justice. All of them were ignored.

Starved of funds and exasperated by the local government's refusal to negotiate, the gang turned to robbing banks. They showed themselves to be experts at this, taking thousands from the National Bank in the small town of Eudora without even firing a shot. During the robbery, they kept 22 locals locked in a storeroom. The victims later told police how the Kelly gang had been polite, considerate, and had even provided a demonstration of their horse-riding skills as a gesture of thanks for the inconvenience they'd caused. The police were not in the least amused.

The next raid was at another bank, in the town of Jerilderie. Once again the gang demonstrated their skills – bank-robbing and horsemanship – to the delight of a large crowd, and Ned gave a speech to the captive townspeople in a hotel dining room. He was growing more ambitious, and even talked of setting up a "republic of Northeast Victoria," where there'd be no squatters, but equality for all. Incensed by Kelly's growing confidence, the police offered a huge reward for his capture and stepped up the persecution of his supporters. Ned decided the time had come to make a last stand.

The gang had already been busy with target practice out in the bush. They shot into trees and then cut the bullets out to reuse them; ammunition was hard to come by in the wilderness. After weeks of practice, they were accomplished marksmen, but Ned knew they'd need a greater advantage over the police than sharpshooting. He wanted his gang to be bulletproof.

Over the next few weeks, the police received complaints from farmers about their tools and crop machinery being stolen in the middle of the night. They didn't pay much attention to the angry farmers. After all, they had the Kelly gang to catch. But it was the gang members who were behind the thefts.

Ned was collecting iron plate. He carried it back to the hideout and painstakingly shaped it into protective suits and helmets. The body plates were heated until they softened and then beaten around a log to make them curved. Smaller plates were welded together to form the helmets, and an eye slit was cut into each one. Nobody is quite sure how Ned got the idea for the iron suits. There were lots of Cantonese miners in the country and it's possible he'd seen samurai suits in a procession during the celebrations for Chinese New Year. Those suits looked a little like the ones he fashioned. But his iron designs were only part of an elaborate plan.

The Kelly gang had decided attack was the best way to defend themselves. On June 27, 1880, they captured the small railway town of Glenrowan, cut the telegraph wires and herded the 30 inhabitants into a small hotel building. Ned knew that the government was sending a special police train up from Melbourne, so he forced a railway engineer to rip up the tracks next to the station. The idea was that, when the police train was derailed, the gang would move up in their suits, attacking any survivors in an open field. In the meantime, a group of their supporters would be waiting in the woods, ready to spread the news that the police were defeated. In Ned's imagination, this victory would be enough to persuade the authorities to grant the gang and his family a fair hearing in court, and perhaps even lead to the setting up of the new, independent state.

Ned Kelly was not lacking in ambition.

For two nights the gang stayed up drinking brandy and chatting with their prisoners, waiting for the train. It would have been wise to rest before the battle, but they were young and confident. They couldn't see how their plan could go wrong. But a young schoolteacher, Thomas Curnow, was horrified at the prospect of the crash, and he managed to sneak out without the gang noticing. He sprinted up the tracks holding a candle as a signal, and alerted the driver of the train. The police jumped to the ground and advanced on the hotel. Inside, the gang quickly donned their metal suits.

They came out shooting. Under a brilliant moon, four iron figures advanced across the field, strafing the 50 policemen with revolver fire. It must have been a monstrous sight. But the gang soon realized the flaw in their plan: the suits were too heavy. At 40kg (90lbs) each, it was like carrying a man on your back, and their charge quickly came to a halt. Also, the parts of their bodies which were unprotected were cut to ribbons by the police bullets. They howled in pain as their feet and hands were smashed and cut. To make matters worse, it was difficult to aim when all they could see was a slice of the moonlit battlefield. Most of their shots went wide, and the police soon drove them back towards the hotel. They lurched inside, bloody and tired, as the police fusillade continued.

Despite the screams from the hostages, many of them women and children, the police kept up their fire. Bullets cut through the hotel's wooden planks and passed out the other side. Each time they hit a gang member's iron chest plate, it was like being punched. When Ned was finally captured, his body was covered in bruises from these "bullet punches." The other gang members never left the hotel alive. At 3:00pm the next day, after the hostages had been set free, the police set fire to the building. Joe Byrne had died the night before, but Dan Kelly and Steve Hart were possibly burned alive.

Even though he'd been badly shot, Ned Kelly survived his wounds and stood trial in the state capital of Melbourne, on October 28, 1880. The judge, Sir Redmond Barry, who had earlier vowed he would see Ned hang, was anxious to get the whole thing over with as quickly as possible. It was the horse-racing season in Melbourne and there were great crowds of visitors in the town. The authorities were concerned there might be a public uprising to save the prisoner.

Ned was only allowed to make a statement after he had been found guilty of the murders that took place at Stringybark Creek. He spoke eloquently and with great passion to defend his actions, adding that he believed there was "a greater court than this," where his actions would be viewed as reasonable.

The judge concluded his grim sentence of "Death by hanging," with the words: "And may the Lord have mercy on your soul."

Ned stared him in the eye and responded: "Yes, I will see you there, where I go."

Despite a petition of 32,000 names to save him, torchlit processions and several notable politicians and lawyers speaking to the state governor on his behalf, Ned was hanged on November 11. His mother's last words to him were: "I'll mind you die like a Kelly, son." He did not disappoint her, remaining calm and in control of his emotions until the end.

Five thousand people gathered outside the prison to mourn Ned Kelly's passing. Twelve days later, Judge Barry died suddenly from natural causes. The proud Australian's grim prediction at his trial had come true.

At war with the world

The usually flint-faced gangster Homer Van Meter was laughing so hard, he almost fell off his barstool. "What did you say?" he asked the kid standing before him.

"I want to join the gang," the kid repeated. "The Dillinger gang. I was told you're one of them."

Van Meter took a sip of his whiskey and studied the boy who had walked over to him at the bar. He was probably in his twenties, but his complexion was so smooth and his cheeks so pudgy, he looked as though he belonged in a nursery. To top it all, he was only just over 1.52m (5ft) tall, and slim too. He was positively puny. Van Meter wasn't in the mood for chatting with an idiot schoolboy. For the last three weeks he'd been on the road, raiding banks with Dillinger's Terror Gang and running from the police. Now he wanted to enjoy his whiskey in peace.

"I don't think so, kid. We rob banks, not candy stores. Go home."

"My name's George Nelson," snarled the boy, through gritted teeth.

"Baby Face Nelson?" Van Meter asked him, in a suddenly hushed voice.

"Some people call me that. Does that change things a little?"

Instinctively, Van Meter crossed his arms to check his gun was in its holster. Reassured by the hard shape at the side of his chest, he slid off his stool and faced the other man.

"You're not laughing now," Nelson whispered.

"People say you're a killer."

"It's no lie," answered Baby Face, with a proud smile.

"And that you enjoy it."

"That's my business," he snapped. "When do I meet Dillinger?"

Van Meter had been in and out of prison for most of his life. He was a career criminal, and had survived beatings, gun battles and months of solitary confinement in the dark emptiness of a prison punishment cell known as "the hole." But, tough as he was, the look in Nelson's eyes sent a shiver down his spine. He braced himself for what he was about to say.

"Nelson, you're too kill-crazy to be in our gang. When we go into a bank we have to be level-headed. We don't shoot unless we have to."

"Are you turning me down?" screamed Baby Face. His fists were bunching and his face flushing red. Van Meter got ready to go for his gun, but Nelson suddenly turned and marched to the door.

"I'll start my own gang," he shouted over his shoulder. "And one day you'll need me. I'll be bigger than Dillinger. You wait and see."

When Nelson was gone, Van Meter hoped he'd seen the last of the pint-sized killer. But much of what Baby Face had promised would come true in the end.

Of all gangster killers, Baby Face Nelson was perhaps the most dangerous. He would kill for the slightest reason, on one occasion shooting a complete stranger who had dared to complain when Nelson scraped his car. It was as though Baby Face was angry with the world and the only time he felt at peace was when his guns were blazing, in the thick of a shoot-out.

He was born Lester Gillis, in the meat-packing district of Chicago, in 1908. His father worked twelve-hour shifts in a factory and his mother had a large family to worry about. Lester was left to wander the streets, and fend for himself.

Those early years scarred the child in body and mind. Lester's diminutive size made him a tempting target for the local bullies. He was hounded and beaten for much of his childhood, until one day he decided he couldn't stand it any longer. Lester became a fighter. What he lacked in stature, he made up for in the ferocity of his attack: Lester Gillis would fight to the death, with knife, rock, club, whatever it took to defeat his opponent. He was fearless. So, the bullied became the bully.

Before long, Lester was leading the kids who had previously taunted him. But he didn't stop there. The violence he had released welled up in a rage against the world. Lester began stealing cars, mocking the police, breaking into houses and stealing from shops. When he was 14, he was caught in a stolen car and sent to a boy's reformatory for two years. In this tough "school for scoundrels," he used his fighting skills to become a leader among the other boys. Lester's fists always got him what he wanted. When he was sent home at 16, he was set in his ways: he would take on the world, and beat it into submission.

After another spell in a reformatory, Lester's reputation as a fighter was such that he was recruited as an enforcer for Al Capone's bootlegging operations. Suddenly he had money, and a taste of the respect that gangsters command by terrorizing their victims. Lester liked his new life, but then came the first hint of his "nemesis" – the flaw in him that would eventually lead to his downfall. His incredible violence had tipped out of control. Lester went too far with the beatings his masters ordered, putting a man in hospital instead of giving him a verbal warning. He was too ready with his guns, and would start shooting over the slightest insult. The gangsters feared their new recruit and, when his actions drew too much attention from the police, they had to act. Lester was lucky though; instead of taking a one-way ride, he was only sacked from the gang.

Dismissing his former masters as cowards, Lester went into business as a one-man gang, stealing precious gems, robbing people at gunpoint and breaking into pawnshop safes. He thought he was invincible, until the police nabbed him in a rare gems store and sent him to Joliet Penitentiary, out on the rolling Chicago plains.

Sitting in his cell, Lester thought things couldn't get much worse. But then his lawyer arrived with news that a witness to one of his armed robberies had contacted the police. He jumped up and rattled the bars.

"How long will I get?" he cried.

"With your record, it could be thirty years," answered the lawyer. "Try to be patient. I'll do what I can."

But Lester wasn't a patient man. The only thing he believed in was the power of his fists. On the train back from the opening hearing of his trial, he feigned illness – possibly by eating cigarette ash, an old convict trick – and when his guard uncuffed him so he could use the bathroom, Lester knocked him down with his knuckles. The train was waiting in a station and the stunned detective could only watch as Lester popped through a carriage window and slid down the embankment to a parked car. His wife, Helen, already had the engine running as he clambered in.

Baby Face had escaped, and he'd be running until the day he died, only two years later.

Lester followed the newspaper editor John Soule's famous advice: "Go west, young man," and pitched up in Sausalito, a small town across the bay from San Francisco. He was sheltered by a local gang boss, Joe Parente, who employed Lester as everything from a parking attendant to a hired killer. Now he was a wanted man, Lester needed a new name. He chose George Nelson, after a boxer he admired. But his baby-faced looks always amused Parente. To Nelson's acute embarrassment, the gang boss would sing the lines from the hit song whenever the two men met:

Baby face, you got the cutest little baby face...

Nelson hated this nickname. The bullies in Chicago had called him this before he earned his gangster reputation. It was only the fact that he needed Parente's protection that stopped him from reaching for his gun.

After a few months, Nelson realized he was going nowhere fast in California. He wanted a chance to be a famous gangster and, at the time, there was no one more famous than John Dillinger, who was marauding across the midwest states. When Nelson met two men who'd worked with Dillinger in the past, machine-gunner Tommy Carroll and jugman Eddie Green, he pestered them for details about their former boss.

The stories they told him whetted his appetite for action. Nelson didn't delay. He packed his suitcase, loaded up the car and drove east with Helen and a friend named John Paul Chase. A few days later, he approached Homer Van Meter in the Indiana saloon.

After he was rebuffed by the Terror Gang, Baby Face set up his own gang. His was a clumsy and violent team of gangsters, and their method of robbing banks was crude compared to the artful Dillinger and his techniques. Baby Face would crash through the bank doors, fire a burst from his machine gun into the ceiling and start shouting orders. He used shock tactics instead of Dillinger's smooth, charming style. But Nelson was effective. A year after the snub in the bar, Van Meter came to see him.

"Dillinger wants you," he muttered. "It's against my wishes, but we're short of men."

It was the chance Nelson had been waiting for. Dillinger was the Most Wanted man in America and now he needed Nelson's help in his gang. Beaming with satisfaction, Nelson shook Van Meter's outstretched hand.

It was the dog days of the Terror Gang when Baby Face Nelson was invited to join. The police "heat" was intense. There was a huge reward for their capture, and the FBI was closing in. But Nelson didn't seem to care. He was on top of the world, robbing banks and toting a machine gun.

From the first raid, Dillinger knew that Baby Face was trouble. While robbing a bank in Sioux Falls, South Dakota, Nelson shot and wounded a policeman. The gang had always tried to avoid firing on the police, as these attacks earned huge jail sentences. Rather than showing any remorse or sense of guilt over endangering his gangster partners, Nelson bragged about the shooting. Dillinger would have dumped his new recruit at once, but there was no one to replace him. Reluctantly, he allowed Nelson to stay in the gang.

During the next raid, in Iowa, Dillinger was shot in the arm by a vigilante sniper. Detectives now trailed the gang from one hideout to the next, and the bank robbers were desperate to find somewhere safe where they could rest and recuperate.

Dillinger took his gang to a remote hotel, the Little Bohemia Lodge, where he hoped to have a week of calm. But, instead of relaxing, Nelson paced the carpet of his lodge cabin, furious about a recent

FBI reward poster he'd seen.

"If you capture Dillinger, you get $10,000," he ranted to Helen. "But I'm only worth half that, according to Hoover. I'm just as dangerous as Dillinger. I should be worth the same reward money."

While the rest of the gang played cards and read magazines, Nelson polished his guns. He would soon need them. The FBI had received a tip-off, and Inspector Melvin Purvis and two carloads of his agents were speeding towards the lodge.

In a bungled fire-fight, three innocent men were shot by the FBI and the gang escaped. Nelson prowled the woods, looking for a house where he might be able to steal a car. When he came across two FBI agents and a local policeman in a patrol car, he turned his guns on them with no warning. One FBI agent died instantly, the other two men were seriously wounded, and Nelson drove off into the night.

There was only one more raid after the Little Bohemia disaster: South Bend, Indiana, on June 30, 1934. It was a blood bath. Homer Van Meter was hit in the side of the head, a policeman died of his wounds and six civilians were injured during a running gun battle. Nelson had been firing wildly, but as usual he escaped without a scratch. Nothing, it seemed, would alter his baby-faced looks.

After South Bend, Nelson decided he would be better off without Dillinger. He went back to

California with Helen, planning to form a new gang of his own. He had been envious of Dillinger's fame for too long. He yearned to be the Most Wanted gangster in America. Only a few weeks later, he would be.

Nelson let out a cheer when he read the newspaper report on July 23, 1934: *Dillinger Ambushed Outside Cinema*. This meant there was a new Public Enemy Number One: Baby Face Nelson. But, only four months later, the FBI caught up with him, leading to one of the most spectacular gun battles in criminal history – in which Baby Face would cement his violent reputation.

Following his gangster promotion, Baby Face had been driven almost insane with rage because the national newspapers and the FBI refused to credit him with the same notoriety as Dillinger. The reward money for Nelson never reached the same heights as it had for the leader of the Terror Gang, and journalists described Nelson as a "punk."

"They'll see who's a punk," fumed Baby Face, "as soon as I start my new gang."

To this end he had been visiting his old haunts in Chicago, trying to find anyone crazy enough to join him. But the word was out: Baby Face was mad, bad and dangerous to know. Nobody wanted anything to do with him.

In the meantime, the FBI had spotted his stolen car using the highways between Chicago and Lake

Geneva, in Wisconsin. Baby Face, Helen and his loyal friend, Chase, were staying in the resorts that dotted this wooded back country. The agent in charge of the operation to catch Nelson, Sam Cowley, ordered 24-hour patrols in the area.

On the afternoon of November 27, 1934, agents William Ryan and Thomas McDade saw a car approaching them on the highway. The registration matched that of Nelson's car.

"Turn it around and get after them," ordered Ryan.

McDade spun the wheel and the FBI car made a U-turn. But Nelson noticed this in his rear-view mirror and it roused his suspicions. He did a U-turn himself, so he could discover who was pursuing him. As the cars flashed past each other, the FBI men saw two men and a woman staring over at them.

"That's Nelson all right," said Ryan. He had been at the Little Bohemia and had heard the sound of Nelson's guns blasting from one of the cabins. Ryan knew they were up against a dangerous man, but he was determined to do his duty. As he stared into the rear-view mirror, working out a plan, he saw Nelson spin his car around again and roar after the FBI car.

"They're coming after us now," shouted McDade.

"That's all right," said Ryan, reassuringly. "We'll get a closer look."

Nelson brought his car up on the right-hand side of the FBI vehicle. The two cars were speeding along at top speed, only inches apart.

"Pull over!" screamed Baby Face through the open window. He was leaning over Helen, who had crouched down in the passenger seat. The FBI men studied their gangster opponent. He was wearing sunglasses and a flat cap, looking for all the world like a polite young man taking his car for a spin in the country. Ryan fingered the revolver in his lap nervously.

"Give it to them!" roared Nelson, and Chase sat up in the rear seat brandishing a powerful rifle. He stuck it through the open window above Helen's shoulder and pulled the trigger. At the same time, Nelson started blasting with an automatic pistol in his left hand, holding the steering wheel with his right. Ryan returned fire, his gun flaming next to McDade's head.

Amazingly, none of the bullets found a human target. The cars were going so fast, it was difficult to aim with any precision. Nelson hit the brakes and let the FBI car pull ahead. McDade pulled over and both agents jumped out, ready for a gunfight, but the gangster's car had vanished. They didn't know it, but a second FBI patrol had seen the battle and was chasing Nelson down another highway. It was the turn of Inspector Cowley and agent Herman Hollis to have a crack at Public Enemy Number One.

After a high-speed pursuit over several miles, the FBI agents were gaining on their quarry. Baby Face cursed as he heard his engine sputtering. One of the bullets had damaged the radiator. He would have to make a stand.

Nelson swung into a field and skidded the car to a halt. Helen ran over to some bushes to hide, while the FBI car raced past into the field, braked hard and stopped next to a shallow ditch. Immediately, bullets from the guns of Nelson and Chase were zinging off its metalwork.

Hollis grabbed a shotgun from the back seat and made it to the ditch. Cowley rescued a machine gun. Both agents were experienced men. Hollis had helped to bring down Dillinger in Chicago and Cowley was a tough, veteran agent, 35 years old and calm under pressure. They were well armed and it was only a question of time before other FBI teams arrived. Cowley must have thought he was in a strong position. But he had never gone up against Baby Face Nelson before.

Both sides were exchanging shots over the middle ground of an open field. In the distance, a group of farm-hands dropped their tools and stared open-mouthed at the shoot-out. Cowley and Hollis were protected by the ditch, Nelson and Chase by their car. It was a gunfight that could have lasted for hours, with neither side having any real advantage. But Nelson didn't believe in drawn-out battles. He grabbed a fresh machine gun, and rushed around the side of the car.

"What are you doing, George?" Chase screamed

after his friend.

"I'm going over there to finish them off," answered Nelson, and stepped out into the open.

Hollis and Cowley couldn't believe their eyes. Baby Face Nelson was striding straight at them, cursing and firing bursts of machine-gun bullets from the hip. There was no cover at all. He was an easy target. Both men took aim and fired.

Bullets tore into his chest, arms and legs, but Baby Face kept advancing.

"Nobody messes with George Nelson!" he screamed, raking the ditch with bullets. His suit was soaked with blood and his body shook each time a shell thudded into him, but Nelson kept coming. He was unstoppable. Cowley and Hollis were shot dead where they lay.

Nelson slumped against the agents' car. "Get this thing started," he shouted back to Chase. Helen came running up from where she'd been hiding and she and Chase helped load Nelson into the front seat.

"Perhaps you should drive," Nelson whispered to his wife, as he closed his eyes.

The next morning the police found his body, wrapped in a blanket, by the gates of a Chicago cemetery 32km (20 miles) from the site of the shoot-out. Incredibly, he had lived for several hours after the gun battle. His wife and best friend had taken him to an underworld doctor for treatment, but his wounds were untreatable. They were both caught and sent to jail: Helen for one year, Chase for 30.

Nelson had been shot 17 times by the FBI agents. His short and violent life had culminated in a last, mad gesture to smash the world. It was the end of the baby-faced killer.

The luckiest gangster alive

If there was one place in the world where gangsters always prospered, it was New York. Al Capone might have ruled Chicago with his bribes and butchery, Las Vegas was Bugsy Siegel's gambling playground for a year or two, and there is no doubt that criminals controlled the Italian cities of Palermo and Naples for decades. But New York was a special place, and it produced a special kind of gangster.

Established in 1629 by Dutch traders (who bought

the land from Native Americans for $24-worth of goods), New York soon became a symbol for all that America had to offer. It was bigger, brighter and richer than other cities. At the beginning of the 20th century, industry and trade were booming in its factories and docks. Wall Street was the heart of the world's financial markets, and business tycoons and the showbiz elite built grand mansions along the Manhattan avenues. New York was the gateway to a new life for tides of migrants, and promised every fresh arrival a world of opportunity and success − if only in their dreams. This made it a magnet for hungry and ambitious people from every walk of life. For the gangster, it represented the ultimate prize. To be gangster king of New York made them the undisputed "boss of bosses." Only a few men ever received this title, and one of them was Charlie Luciano. He was, by some accounts, the most successful gangster in history, and he was certainly one of the luckiest.

Luciano first saw the New York skyline from the deck of a transatlantic steamer when he was only nine years old. He'd been born with the first name Salvatore, which he changed to the more American-sounding Charlie after spending a few years in the city. He didn't get his nickname, "Lucky," until he was in his twenties. In fact, his parents didn't think their little boy had been lucky at all. Like tens of thousands of their countrymen, they had emigrated to escape the crushing poverty of rural life in Sicily, Italy. Luciano's father was a digger in the chemical mines not far from Palermo. But even with this job, it was hard to feed his family on the wages he earned. The parents worried about Salvatore's prospects. Surely the move to the glittering streets of America would give them a better quality of life and a choice of careers for their son.

But life in the Big Apple came as a shock. There were opportunities in New York, but not the kind Luciano's parents had hoped for. They arrived in 1906 and, within a year, Salvatore had his first brush with the law; he was arrested for shoplifting. Salvatore wasn't interested in school or finding a job. There were other, less painful ways to get rich. He'd seen the well-dressed Sicilian men in his street, with their fancy cars and polished leather shoes. If he followed them around, they sometimes asked him to run a message or fetch them a cup of coffee. When he returned, they'd hand him a "sawbuck" (a $10 bill) as a tip – more than his father could earn in a whole week. These men were known as "wise guys" and they preyed on the poor Italian immigrant communities in New York, just as they had done in the old country. They were gangsters.

The same criminal parasites who plagued the poor in Italy had followed the ships across the ocean. This was the "Mafia": a network of criminal gangs who had been active in Europe for centuries. Their organization was so shadowy that it's impossible to describe in detail. Even the origin of their name is a mystery. However, the Mafia relied on two membership rules: *omerta*, or "silence," to make sure that nobody talked to the police; and absolute loyalty to the gang boss. Breaking either rule had fatal consequences.

The New York Mafia was a collection of Sicilian gangsters. But there were thousands of other gangsters in the city, drawn from all over the world. The youthful Salvatore was only tolerated by the local wise guys because he was a Sicilian – one of them.

The wise guys' money-making schemes and rackets included gambling dens, money-lending and control of the Italian workforce in the factories and docks. The docklands were a real treasure-house for the gangs. At least ten percent of every cargo would be "taxed" by the wise guys – and if the owner didn't like it and made a complaint, the next time he came in to port there would be no one to unload his ship. If that didn't persuade him to pay up, he might get a visit in the middle of the night from a man with a gun. So few people complained.

Another gangster racket was extortion. Wise guys would demand money from an individual or a company, using threats and violence if necessary. If they already had a gangster reputation, they could just walk into a shop and ask for "protection" money.

"Protection from what?" the owner might joke.

"Damages," the wise guy would answer, pulling down a shelf loaded with valuable produce or dropping a lit match on the floor. The fear of attack or arson would encourage the shop owner to pay a weekly protection charge.

Other extortion techniques were more furtive. Salvatore listened carefully as one wise guy told him about the old "Black Hand" racket.

An Italian immigrant, usually a wealthy businessman or shop owner, would receive a letter. It might just say: *We are watching you.* At the bottom, there would be a drawing of a black hand instead of a signature. The next day another letter would arrive, giving a few more details: *We have decided you have too much money. The Black Hand wants some of it, so get ready to pay.* Again, it would be signed with the same menacing drawing.

For a week or two, the letters would come every day. Victims grew increasingly desperate, looking over their shoulder all the time in case they were being followed, terrified one of their family might be kidnapped or hurt by the Black Hand – whoever, or whatever, it might be. Finally, a letter with a specific demand would arrive: *Tomorrow, give $10,000 to the man with the red tie, carrying a white rose.*

The next morning, a man fitting this description would be waiting in the street. The victim would hand him a roll of dollar bills in an envelope, and the man would smile and walk away. Then the letters would stop. For a while, at least.

Of course, some brave people stood up to the Black Hand racket. When the wise guy came to collect the money, they refused. But there would be immediate and violent repercussions. If the victim owned a shop, it might be burned. Or he might be beaten with clubs, stabbed, or even "garrotted" – strangled with a piece of piano wire. If they still refused to pay, they were taken on a one-way ride. The Black Hand never backed down. In common with all Mafia rackets, its success relied on fear being maintained in the community it terrorized.

Salvatore didn't pay attention to the teachers at school but he never forgot his Black Hand lesson. The technique of using fear and overwhelming force to get what he wanted was behind everything he did in later life.

When Salvatore was ten, he started his first extortion racket, offering protection to boys on their way to school. Luciano charged a penny a day and, if they didn't pay up at once, he gave them a beating. But one kid, wiry and small, told him he didn't need protection. When Luciano attacked, the kid fought back like a tiger. Exhausted and impressed, Luciano asked his name.

"Meyer Lansky," the boy replied, "and don't you ever forget it."

Luciano never would. The two boys became firm friends. They were already street-tough, adolescent gangsters and prospective gang leaders. Over the next ten years, they rapidly learned their criminal trade, robbing houses, staging robberies and running rackets, until the age of Prohibition made them rich.

In their early twenties, the pair drew up plans for a union of gangsters – the Syndicate. Charlie, as he now called himself, was a forceful gang leader, ruthless and violent. Lansky was more calculating; he was the brain compared to Luciano's brawn. Known by his closest friends as "Little Man," he ran a gang with Bugsy Siegel, the impulsive and stylish gangster who later became famous for turning Las Vegas into a gambler's paradise (Bugsy's story is told in "Desert Dreamer" on pages 45-59).

Luciano and Lansky wanted to get the Syndicate up and running, with Luciano as the gangster king of New York. They understood that if the gangs cooperated, they would all become richer and more powerful. But there were some formidable obstacles standing in their way. Joe "the Boss" Masseria and Salvatore Maranzano were two rival gang leaders who both wanted to be the boss of bosses. Together, they ran New York. But soon they would wage gangster war against each other. Charlie was about to earn his nickname.

Masseria and Maranzano were old-fashioned wise guys, known as "Moustache Petes." This was a reference to traditional Sicilian gangsters, who had very fixed ideas about how the Mafia should be run. Some of these old-boys really did have long moustaches. They'd seen Luciano get rich from the illegal alcohol trade and wanted a piece of the action. But Charlie didn't respect his elders. In his opinion, the Moustache Petes were too set in their ways. They opposed the new rackets of drugs and vice on moral grounds. Worse than this, they refused to deal with any non-Sicilians. Luciano had many friends and gangster colleagues, including Lansky, who were Jews. All Charlie cared about was making money, and he thought the old Sicilian gangsters were fools to be so prejudiced. Secretly, Charlie and Lansky decided that both bosses would have to go – but, in the meantime, they supported Masseria. Lansky had calculated that Masseria would be the winner.

When the war started, it was known as the "Castellemmarese War," after the name of Maranzano's birth village. The months passed and wise guys were being gunned down on both sides. But then, it began to look as though Maranzano was getting the upper hand. Luciano made plans to change sides if Lansky had backed the wrong horse. So far, Luciano had managed to avoid the violence himself. Then, one afternoon, he was bundled into the back of a car by four brutes in suits.

"Where are we going?" he screamed.

"On a one-way ride," growled one of his captors.

They drove out to a deserted warehouse where Charlie was tortured and beaten. At one point his face was slashed with a knife, and the muscles under his cheek were severed. The gangster closed his eyes and prepared himself for death. Nobody comes back from a one-way ride.

When he woke with the sound of the wind and the surf in his ears, Luciano wondered if he was in the afterlife. Then he felt his face throbbing and, when he touched his cheek, he could feel the open wound. He looked around and saw that he was on a beach, across the water from the Manhattan skyscrapers. It was the same view he'd first had of New York, 25 years earlier. He managed to stagger to the highway, where he was picked up by a police car and rushed to the hospital.

Charlie had survived a one-way ride. He was the luckiest gangster alive, and he'd earned his nickname.

It was never clear who was behind the attack on Luciano. Maranzano might have ordered it because Charlie was refusing to assassinate Masseria and join his side. Or perhaps Masseria had grown suspicious of his gangster "lieutenant." Whoever was responsible, Charlie wasn't taking any chances. The knife wound he suffered had cut the nerves around his right eye and the eyelid drooped. It was a permanent reminder of how close he'd come to death.

Six months after the failed hit, Charlie took Masseria to a Coney Island restaurant. They had an extravagant meal, discussed the future of the gang and played a hand of cards. When Charlie excused himself to go to the bathroom, four men rushed in from the street and blasted Masseria to pieces.

The jubilant Maranzano immediately named himself boss of bosses. He held a banquet in New York and invited 500 wise guys to celebrate the news. He made Luciano his lieutenant, and then made plans to assassinate him. Charlie was too much of a threat to the old traditions of the Sicilian Mafia. Maranzano ordered him to a meeting at his downtown apartment. Lurking behind the door of the apartment was Vincent "Mad Dog" Coll. Coll had been a member of the Dutch Schultz gang but, after a falling-out, he'd turned his hand to contract killing to earn a living. Maranzano had paid him to kill Lucky as soon as he arrived for the meeting.

As Coll waited with his gun, Maranzano walked over to his office, to give himself an alibi for Lucky's imminent murder. He was expecting an interview with some detectives from the tax office, which would give him a solid alibi. When five men in suits walked into his rooms, Maranzano assumed they were tax accountants and politely offered them a seat. Two of them pushed him back onto his desk and shot him in the head.

Luciano and Lansky had been one step ahead of the last of the Moustache Petes. As Maranzano was blasted in his office, a series of assassinations was carried out across the country. Up to 20 gangsters with old time Sicilian values were "rubbed out," to make way for the Syndicate. Mad Dog Coll escaped, but was gunned down a few months later as he stood in a phone booth.

At a Syndicate meeting a few weeks later, Lansky explained to Bugsy Siegel: "I didn't make a mistake about who to support in the Castellemmarese War. I supported Lucky Luciano from the beginning. Everyone else had to die."

The Black Hand lessons of threat and force had served Luciano well. For five years he reigned supreme as the gangster boss of New York. He lived in a luxury suite at a five-star hotel, ate at the best restaurants and mingled with showbiz stars and sportsmen. Thanks to the efficiency and ready violence of the Syndicate, he received a percentage from every racket in town. Even if a gangster wanted to commit a $10 robbery or open a tiny gambling den, they had to make an appointment to see Lucky Luciano and get his permission.

But the good times couldn't last. For the gangster, the deadliest risk of all is celebrity. The fewer people who know who you are and what you do to make your money, the better your chances of survival. Smart gangsters – like Meyer Lansky – went about their business quietly, trying not to attract too much attention. But Lucky was always in the news.

In 1936, an ambitious District Attorney, Thomas Dewey, wanted to show that he was the real power in New York. He managed to prove in court that Lucky had been living off "illegal earnings." Luciano was stunned when he was sentenced to 30 to 50 years in prison. He was even more shocked when he learned that he was being sent to Dannemora, known by convicts as the "Siberian prison," as it was close to the border with Canada and whipped by freezing winds.

It wasn't all bad news for Lucky though. He didn't have all the luxuries he was used to, but he was allowed as many visitors as he wanted. Lansky was a regular caller, proving his loyalty to his old friend. And Lucky never lost control of the New York gangs. From inside his prison cell he continued to make all the final decisions about gang business. He kept up with the news of the rackets and always checked that a share of their proceeds was paid into his bank account.

But, of course, he was also racking his brains for a way to get out of prison and in 1941, after the outbreak of the Second World War, he got his chance.

As soon as America entered the war, military planners started looking for a way to invade German-controlled Europe. Lucky requested an interview with the army, and craftily explained that he might be a useful ally if they were thinking of advancing through Sicily. Luciano was well-connected in Italy. He knew that Italy's Fascist dictator, Benito Mussolini, had been cracking down on the Mafia for years before the war, and the local gangsters would be happy to help the Americans attack him – for a price, of course. In return for Lucky helping the Allied war effort by organizing Mafia missions of sabotage and espionage, perhaps the army could put in a good word with the New York authorities, and get him out of prison?

Luciano's proposal didn't impress the army. They were reluctant to have anything to do with a convicted gangster. But this wasn't the only card up the wise guy's sleeve.

Next, he contacted the navy and told them of the threat of enemy sabotage around the New York docks. As if to prove his point, a French liner, the *SS Normandie*, was set on fire by "persons unknown." Luciano assured the navy that he could guarantee security around the docks with his army of gangsters, who of course had nothing to do with the attack on the French ship. The navy was grateful for Lucky's patriotic assistance.

At the end of the war, and with no trouble reported in New York's docks, Luciano's request for parole was sent to his old enemy, Dewey, who was now Governor of New York. Dewey had no intention of letting Luciano return to his gangster throne in the city, but he thought there might be another way to reward him for his help during the war. He offered to free Luciano – but only on the condition that he returned to Italy and stayed there for good.

Lucky was so certain he'd be able to slip back into America, he accepted the offer. On February 10, 1946, the middle-aged gangster was taken to Ellis

Island, where he would have arrived as a young immigrant almost 40 years earlier, and shipped back to his homeland. The cream of America's criminals were standing on the dock to wave him off. Some of them were even weeping, but these were crocodile tears. Luciano had become a kind of Moustache Pete in his turn. Now, there was a new, hungry generation of gangsters waiting impatiently for their chance to be king.

For 15 years, Luciano lived in the suburbs of Naples, Italy, biding his time before he could return to New York in glory. It never happened. He made a desperate voyage to Cuba, hoping to slip into Florida from there, but was deported as soon as he stepped off the ship. Apart from that, Luciano never got close to America. The Italian authorities kept a close watch on him. He even had to ask permission to leave the city borders and entertain foreign guests. One of these guests was a scriptwriter who was flying into town to talk with Lucky about making a film of his life. On January 26, 1962, Luciano was at the airport to meet the writer. As he rushed over to greet him, Lucky suffered a huge heart attack and died on the spot.

By that time, even his relationship with Lansky had become strained, and there were some gangsters who whispered that Lucky's heart attack was no accident. The Mafia had always been publicity-shy and it's possible someone slipped poison into Lucky's coffee at the airport, to stop him from going ahead with the film. But his heart was already weak and it seems likely he died of natural causes.

Only in death was Luciano allowed to return to his beloved America. The lucky gangster was buried in a New York cemetery, in a lavish mausoleum.

The gangster who beat "the Rock"

When the FBI finally tracked "Ma" and Freddie Barker to their ramshackle hideout in the Florida Everglades, it was all thanks to a 4.5m (15ft) alligator called "Old Joe." One of their informants had told them a story about Alvin "Old Creepy" Karpis and the alligator. Old Joe lived in a lake, situated next to a hideout Karpis was using. For months, the beast had been menacing the countryside and Karpis had bragged about how he was going to catch it. The FBI knew that Karpis had close links to the Barker gang. If they could find Old Joe's lake, there was a good chance they'd find the Barkers. When FBI agents arrested another gang member, "Doc" Barker, in Chicago, they found a map in his pocket with a ring of ink marking a small lake. They studied the map and planned their raid.

The duel between Karpis and Old Joe reveals a lot about the character of the gangster, the last criminal to be declared Public Enemy Number One. Old Joe had been stalking the cabin for weeks, hoping for an easy snack, but none of the Barker gang could think of a way to kill him. They tried shooting from the lake shore with hunting rifles, but Old Joe was too clever. He simply sank beneath the surface as soon as they started to take aim. Karpis approached the problem in his customary, cool and calculating fashion. He was a keen fisherman. Why not fish for the 'gator? So, the resourceful gangster stole a pig from a local farmer and tied a length of rope around its middle. Then he towed the squealing porker behind a motor boat, circling the lake. It was just like going fishing, except the bait was a 90kg (200lb) pig and he was out to catch an alligator. Karpis and Freddie Barker armed themselves with machine guns, and got ready to surprise Old Joe as soon as he popped up to grab his lunch.

Of course, the wily alligator wasn't taken in by this scheme and didn't take the bait. Karpis was going up against one of the most skilful predators nature has ever produced, and lost. But it was still an ingenious, if slightly crazy, bit of planning. Alvin was an unusual gangster, more of a thinker than a man of action. His ability to sift through plans and weigh up their faults and merits made him one of the most efficient gangsters of his age. For five years, he was always one step ahead of the police, robbing banks and kidnapping millionaires for hefty ransoms. He even hijacked a mail train. It was his meticulous attention to the details of every plan that made him Public Enemy Number One – and which also helped him to beat the toughest prison in the world: Alcatraz.

Alvin Karpis had his own ideas about what made a successful gangster. "You need brains and style, and a cool, hard way of handling yourself," he explained to a friend. He wasn't physically strong or imposing; other criminals were surprised when they met him and saw how skinny he was. But he had a penetrating, dead-eyed stare that could terrify the most hardened gangsters. It was this stare that earned him his sinister nickname.

Alvin "Old Creepy" Karpis was born in Montreal, Canada, in 1908, to Lithuanian parents. The family soon moved to Kansas, and by the time Alvin was ten, he was doing chores for local crooks. He found it exciting, spending his days with people his parents didn't approve of. Perhaps he never intended to become a gangster himself but, after committing a series of petty crimes, he wound up in prison. This could have been an opportunity for Karpis to mull things over and decide on making a fresh start in life after his release. But unfortunately his term behind bars coincided with that of a charismatic and deadly career criminal: Freddie Barker. The two young men became close friends and, when they walked out of prison in 1931, Freddie asked Karpis to join his gang.

The Barker gang consisted of four brothers: Freddie, Arthur, better known as "Doc," Herman and Lloyd. It was a violent and lawless family. Herman was already dead when Karpis arrived on the scene. He'd been in a gunfight with Kansas highway police and had shot himself with his Luger pistol rather than surrender. Lloyd was serving 25 years for robbery. (When he finally got out in 1949, he was shot dead by his own wife.) Doc and Freddie still lived with their mother, Arizona Barker, who was known to everyone as "Ma." She was old and wizened, but fiercely protective of her boys. This included Old Creepy, whom she treated like an adopted son.

Karpis, Freddie and Doc formed the nucleus of the gang. They recruited other gangsters as hired help when a job called for more than three men. Their first bank raid brought them $112,000. The gang carried army-issue machine guns and didn't hesitate to use them. On the way out of the bank, they stumbled into two policemen and an unlucky bystander; all three were shot dead in an instant.

For a year the gang smashed their way into bulletproof cars and bank safes, grabbing hundreds of thousands of dollars. But it was a dangerous occupation. Several of the hired gangsters died in shoot-outs with the police. When the banks began hiring armed security guards, the gang decided to try their hand at kidnapping. This was lucrative and seemed less risky, but kidnapping was a federal (national) crime. Suddenly, the FBI was hunting the gang down. After they arrested Doc, they surrounded the hideout in Florida and, in a blizzard of gunfire, both Freddie and Ma were killed. Freddie had 16 bullets in his body.

The newspapers tried to present Ma as one of the gang, saying she had been active in organizing the crimes and that she deserved to die in the shoot-out. But Karpis later claimed she was a doting mother, and nothing more. "Organize a robbery? She couldn't organize a breakfast," joked another gangster.

The Florida gunfight marked the end of the gang. Doc languished in the eerie silence of Alcatraz while Karpis, who had been away from the hideout on a fishing trip, went into hiding. For over a year he fought an exhausting and hopeless battle of wills with the Director of the FBI, J. Edgar Hoover. Karpis expected to be shot on sight, and he was running for his life. But Hoover was under pressure too. The Director had been ridiculed by politicians over the fact that he had never personally made an arrest. Hoover was determined to get the credit for capturing Karpis himself.

Old Creepy was finally nabbed on May 1, 1936, when one of the FBI's informers betrayed him in New Orleans. He was arrested as he walked out of his apartment and climbed into a car. FBI agents were just about to storm the building when the gangster appeared. They hadn't expected to take him alive. Hoover claimed that he put the handcuffs on Old Creepy himself – but in reality the Director was hiding down the street, waiting for the all-clear before making his appearance. In their excitement, none of the FBI agents had remembered to bring any handcuffs. So a necktie was used to secure Alvin's hands instead. Karpis offered the cops his own tie, but they decided against it.

The gangster was found guilty of kidnapping and sent to Alcatraz prison for life. He was 27 years old. So fearsome was the reputation of the island penitentiary, nobody expected him to survive the sentence.

While Karpis had been racing around the country, dodging the FBI, Doc Barker had concentrated his energies and been busy on "the Rock" – as Alcatraz was known. Doc was a small, wiry man, only 1.6m (5ft 3in) tall, but his forceful character made him a natural leader among the prison's killers and thieves. He had assembled a gang of trusted men to help with his scheme. Barker was planning the impossible: an escape from Alcatraz.

When Karpis arrived, he urged his old friend to be cautious. Old Creepy knew about water. As well as the sharks and freezing temperatures in the tides around the island, there were hidden currents that could pull a man out into the raging waters of the Pacific Ocean in minutes.

As if to prove his point, on December 17, 1937, Theodore Cole and Ralph Roe broke out of a work room and ran down to the shore. A light fog covered the bay, but Karpis could see the escape attempt from his own work space. He saw the two men pull crude rubber floats over their arms. They'd made the floats from door mats, to help them with the long swim to the mainland. Karpis watched them slip into the icy water and paddle away. Like a patient fisherman quietly tending his line, Karpis studied the desperate swimmers. Soon, they were struggling against a powerful undertow that threatened to pull them below the waves. Finally, Karpis turned away from the window and went back to his work.

When Barker asked him if he thought the two men had made it to the shore, Karpis was curt: "Of course not. If you want to get out of this place alive,

I hope your plan's better than theirs."

Cole and Roe were never found, although some of the prisoners joked that each year the warden received a postcard from South America, bearing their signatures. But Karpis wasn't impressed: he was sure he'd seen them drowning as they drifted towards the fog.

Things happened slowly on Alcatraz. It took Doc two and a half years to complete his escape plan. As soon as all the details were ready, he asked Karpis for his expert opinion.

Doc still believed the best chance for escape was to swim across the bay to San Francisco. He thought Cole and Roe had failed because they didn't have the right equipment. As well as having better floats, Doc's gang had fitted a metal dust mask with rubber pipes and bits of wire, and transformed it into a snorkel mask. With this piece of kit, there was less risk of drowning during the crossing. If a man was sucked underwater, he could still breathe and fight his way back to the surface. Another part of the plan was for the escape team of five men to build rafts out of the driftwood that routinely washed up on the Alcatraz beaches. They would use the sheets from their cell beds to lash the wood together. If the water wasn't too choppy, they might get to the mainland without even getting their feet wet.

Karpis studied Doc's plan for two weeks, then gave his verdict.

"It won't work. If they don't shoot you, you'll all drown."

"Thanks," snarled Doc, "and I suppose you've got a better idea?"

Karpis smiled and nodded his head. "Naturally."

Old Creepy was just as desperate to break out of prison as his friend. He'd used his time on the Rock carefully, studying every detail of his environment: the buildings, the guards, even the warden. Now he had a plan that was different from any previous escape attempt, and twice as daring.

The gang would wait for a foggy night, then break out of their cells. Doc already knew how to bend the cell bars using a special tool he'd smuggled into the prison in the body of a guitar. But, instead of running to the water as Doc intended, they would hide in the cell block. When the night patrol came around to check on the sleeping prisoners, the gang would overpower them, tie them up and steal their guns and uniforms. Dressed as guards, and with their faces hidden by darkness and fog, they could stroll over to the family compound where all the prison staff and their families lived. After all, who would think of challenging them in their uniforms? The next stage was to knock on the front door of the warden's house.

"You really are crazy," snorted Doc. "What do you want with the warden?"

Karpis explained that once the warden and his

family were tied up, the gang would send for the prison doctor. When he arrived, he would be grabbed and tied up with the others.

"And how does that help us?" asked Doc in a mocking tone.

The next part of the Karpis plan was ingenious. He described how they would force the doctor to speak with the guards at the boathouse. He'd order them to prepare the prison's motor launch. Using the cover story that the warden's wife needed an emergency operation on the mainland, the gang and their hostages would march down to the quay and climb into the waiting boat. The doctor couldn't possibly refuse to cooperate when he saw the gangsters had guns. Once they were all aboard, they could pilot the boat to anywhere on the Californian coast.

It was an original and inventive plan. Doc rejected it instantly.

"Too complicated," he spat. "And there'll be at least eight of us trying to get into the boat. What if one of the guards is suspicious of all those people?"

"Then we've got hostages and guns," replied Karpis. "We could shoot our way down to the dock and take the boat by force."

But Doc Barker wouldn't listen. The Karpis plan struck him as silly and unworkable. He'd already decided his own plan was fail-safe. From then on, the two friends knew that their former allegiance was over. Karpis thought it was for the best. He wasn't interested in any escape that used Doc's plan. After studying it carefully, he'd seen it was doomed to end in failure. The veteran fisherman was right.

Early in the morning of January 13, 1939, Doc and four of his gang crept out of their cell block and down to a secluded beach. The height of the waves and their bone-chilling temperatures took the men by surprise. They were used to staring down onto the surf from the prison buildings, where it appeared flat and calm. At sea level, the bay looked like a cauldron of boiling water. But Doc wasn't turning back now. The gang built a fragile raft and clambered aboard.

Twice they ventured out into that rough, winter sea. Twice they paddled back to shore and tried to make their raft more sturdy. The gang was amazed by the strength of the currents and the violence of the waves washing over them. They concentrated all their efforts on building a stronger craft. It was so noisy down on the beach, Doc and his gang didn't hear the siren howling in the air above them.

A guard had discovered their abandoned cells on a routine check. He sounded the alarm and the whole island was suddenly swarming with guards and searchlights. The prison launch – the escape vehicle for the Karpis plan – circled the island with its spotlight sweeping the surf, a machine-gunner standing ready in the prow. As the boat rounded a cliff, the captain spotted two men on the beach, working on a raft. It was Doc and a man named

Stamphill. They tried to make a run for it but were machine-gunned in the legs. In an effort to hide, they crawled behind a large rock. Meanwhile, the other three gangsters were caught farther up the beach, where they'd been sent to look for more driftwood.

When Doc poked his head above the rock to see if the coast was clear, he was hit in the forehead by another machine-gun bullet. This was too much for Stamphill. He jumped to his feet and lifted his arms in surrender.

Guards ran up the beach, loaded the dying gangster into the launch and ferried him back to the dock. Doc Barker died later that afternoon. His last words were: "I was a fool to try it. I'm all shot to hell."

Karpis had lost the last of his old friends, a man he loved like a brother. For weeks he mooched in his cell, but then he decided there was only one way to have his revenge: he would beat the Rock. Old Creepy would sit out his sentence, and leave the island a free man. To this end, he put all thoughts of escape out of his mind and worked hard at his job in the prison bakery. The former bank robber and machine-gunner became renowned for his delicious cupcakes. His hard work at the ovens won him the praise of the parole board and prison officials. They'd forgotten how crafty Old Creepy was; he brewed beer with the yeast he was given to make bread and cakes. A glass of ale helped to pass the time...

After serving an incredible 33 years in prison – 25 of them in Alcatraz, longer than any other inmate – he was paroled in 1969 and deported to Canada, his birthplace. Four years later, he moved to the Costa del Sol in Spain, and passed the rest of his days quietly, giving the occasional interview to criminologists.

Old Creepy outlived Hoover, who died in his sleep in 1972. He also outlived most of his gangster contemporaries, who had perished under police fire, in car chases, or in prison as old men, shuffling about in their slippers. Karpis sipped red wine and went fishing in his retirement.

But there was a last twist in the old gangster's story. In 1979, he was found dead in his apartment. At an inquest, the coroner declared that Karpis had died of an overdose of prescription drugs. There was an open verdict: nobody knows if Old Creepy took his own life or met with a more sinister end.

Also from Usborne True Stories

TRUE STORIES OF
CRIME &
DETECTION

GILL HARVEY

On a wind-blasted, stormy night in August 1998, the people who lived next to Hyde cemetery got the fright of their lives... a caretaker at the retirement home overlooking the cemetery saw something that made his blood run cold.

"There are people with shovels in the graveyard," he whispered into his telephone, "and they're digging around the tombs. Send for the police."

He almost dropped the receiver when he heard the reply: "But that is the police, sir."

Are real criminals and detectives anything like the ones you read about in novels or see on the television? You can find out in these ten exciting stories. Serial murderers, art forgers, kidnappers, robbers, runaways and forensic scientists are all here, as well as cases of real-life horror that will chill you to the bone.

TRUE
SPY
STORIES

Paul Dowswell & Fergus Fleming

"In all your years of fame," Kramer explained delicately, "you have known some of the most powerful men in Europe. Would you consider returning to Paris now to mingle again with these influential gentlemen? And, while you're doing this, might you be able to keep me informed of anything interesting they might say?"

Margaretha looked curious but non-committal.

Kramer went on, "We could pay you well for this information — say 24,000 francs."

What are real spies like? Some, like beautiful Mata Hari, are every bit as glamorous as famous fictional agents such as James Bond. But spies usually live shadowy double lives, risking prison, torture and execution for a chance to change history.

TRUE
ESCAPE
STORIES
Paul Dowswell

Finally, the night had come to take a trip to the roof. Morris spent the day beforehand trying to curb his restlessness. What if the way up to the roof was blocked? What if the ventilator motor had been replaced after all? All their painstaking work would be wasted. The 12-year sentence stretched out before him. Then another awful thought occurred. The holes in the wall would be discovered eventually, and that would mean even more years added on to his sentence.

As well as locked doors, high walls and barbed wire, many escaping prisoners also face savage dogs and armed guards who shoot to kill. From Alcatraz to Devil's Island, read the extraordinary tales of people who risked their lives for their freedom.